FEARLESS PURPOSE

Training with the Uncertainty & Anxiety
of Your Meaningful Work

LEO BABAUTA

Published by Pipe Dreams Publishing, in San Diego.

This book is uncopyrighted. The author and publisher release all rights to the work contained herein. Freely use the text as you like.

DEDICATION

I dedicate this book to the Founding Members of my Fearless Mastery mastermind group. They said Hell Yes to my invitation to create massive shifts for ourselves, to practice with our patterns and deepen into our purposes.

They are a group of amazing leaders who are changing the world. It is one of the greatest honors of my life to be working with them, and my teammates Coyote and Phil.

Aili: An incredible spirit, I've come to appreciate Aili's tender heart, her love for anyone struggling with self-compassion, and the depth of her practice.

Ales: One of the most playful people I know, Ales brings a great love of knowledge, a great willingness to train, and a fantastic curiosity that serves everyone he comes into contact with.

Amanda: There's something breathtaking about her willingness to leap into the unknown, despite feeling shaky and doubtful, that inspires everyone around her. She's destined to do great things.

Ann: A lifelong achiever and leader, Ann discovered and demonstrated the value of letting yourself be tenderized by heartbreak, and the absolute freedom of letting go.

Brittany: As someone who cannot stand for injustice, Brittany is a powerful leader who feels intensely and cares tremendously. She's a force the world will have no choice to reckon with, and will be better off because of it.

Christoph: A man who brings a refreshing openness and energy to every room he enters, Christoph has a childlike nature that can only open the hearts of those around him. He brings goodness into the world.

Davor: He lives life fully, as few people do. He's got a beautiful soul and a lot to offer, and when he finds his path, look out.

Diane: One of the most dynamic people you'll ever meet, Diane lights up every room, bringing joy to the world, music and dance, laughter and togetherness. She is a beacon of positive energy, and displays an unmatched tenderness in her heart.

Eric: A powerful entrepreneur, Eric is the rare achiever who isn't satisfied with accomplishment, but demands to go deeper, and is willing to change everything in service of living his best life.

Erik: There are few people who have been hit harder by life's tragedies and challenges, while still having such a huge smile on his face. He has overcome more than anyone should ever have to face, and his incredible heart and dedication have been a source of personal inspiration to me.

Ian: Most people would be satisfied with the stunning success that Ian has created in his life, but he isn't content to stop there — he wants to be a powerful force for justice and good in the world. He feels such a strong sense of responsibility, and heartfelt desire to help others, that we are lucky to have him working with us.

Katherine: She's such a powerful doer and thinker, and is applying the full force of her being to changing the world, to tackling the daunting problem of climate change, by empowering those who work in the field to magnify their forces.

Leslie: There isn't a bigger heart in the world, who cares about the caretakers, the anxious and overwhelmed, the animals of the world in need. She works tirelessly to serve others, and has a seemingly endless supply of love.

Nick: His willingness to bring his vulnerability, even when it's scary, will just knock you to the floor. It's a vulnerability that inspires others, and that will change many lives.

Raphael: A man who has overcome innumerable obstacles to bring mindfulness, health, practice, focus, and service into his life.

Robrecht: This is someone who dares to envision an incredible new future, in which we tap into ancient wisdom, come together for the possibility of peace, revive oral traditions and the spirit of festivals, and create connection and presence in a joyful way.

Suraj: A beautiful human being who has serving others at the core of his being, Suraj is willing to go deep, willing to be present with and listen to anyone, willing to open to his fears, willing to learn with a delightful enthusiasm, willing to pour vast compassion from his heart.

Ville: He dances with his fears, is willing to toss out respectability for powerful possibility, and will move mountains to create a monastery in his city to impact the lives of others. He's willing to meditate on death to help realize the truth of impermanence, and I love him for it.

Fearless Training team leaders: In addition, this book is also dedicated to the team leaders in the Fearless Training Program . . . past, present and future. Without them, we could not have the incredible community that has grown in the program, supporting each other's training. This book wouldn't exist without them, and we are eternally grateful for their tireless, devoted service to their teams.

CONTENTS

Preface 1
Introduction 3
Chapter 1: The Problem 7
Chapter 2: The Opportunity 13
Chapter 3: The Training 15
Chapter 4: The Shift 19
Chapter 5: Depth of Purpose 23
Chapter 6: The Deeper Love 29
Chapter 7: The Container 33
Chapter 8: The Training Session
    & the Fearless Practice 39
Chapter 9: Calling Out Patterns 45
Chapter 10: Hold the Pose to Shift the Patterns 51
Chapter 11: Cultivating Fearlessness,
    Gentleness, Friendliness 55
Chapter 12: Common Obstacles 59
Chapter 13: Adjusting the Training 67
Chapter 14: Falling in Love with the Moment 71
Chapter 15: Relaxing Into the Openness 77
Chapter 16: Increasing the Intensity 83
Chapter 17: Finding Joy & Gratitude 91
Chapter 18: Deepening Integrity 95
Chapter 19: Deepening Focus 101
Chapter 20: Deepening into Emptiness 109
Chapter 21: Cultivating Mastery of Purpose 115
Chapter 22: The Training Program 121
Indebtedness & Acknowledgements 129

FEARLESS PURPOSE

Preface

As I write these words, preparing to send this book to print, we are at the end of Summer 2020, and hoo boy. What a year it's been.

Our lives are always filled with uncertainty and some level of anxiety, but the pandemic of this year has taken it to another level. Many levels, actually.

Uncertainty and fear are so in-our-faces that we have no choice but to notice how we respond. We seek comfort, we judge others in frustration, we look for the exits, we scramble frantically trying to get control, we procrastinate and distract ourselves.

The good news is that this intense uncertainty is *the perfect opportunity to practice*.

When we notice how crazy we're feeling from the uncertainty of this year . . . we can turn towards it.

We can practice with it.

We can notice what we habitually do. And practice something different. We can practice mindfulness and openness and gratitude and focus.

We can deepen even further into our purpose.

It's a beautiful time to be alive and practice. The methods and practices in this book are even more important than ever.

I invite you to deepen into it with me.

Leo Babauta

Introduction

I wish I could show you...
the astonishing light of your own being.

~HAFEZ

Our world is full of bustling busyness, plentiful comforts, incredible distractions.

And while you might think this would lead to greater ease and comfort, it actually yields the opposite. We train our minds to run to these comforts and distractions, to default to busyness, so that we can avoid uncertainty and discomfort. But it doesn't lead to happiness — in fact, it leads to procrastination, unhealthy lifestyles, financial messes, and a life of wasting our precious hours.

What if instead of busyness, we slowed down and found focus and purpose?

What if instead of seeking comfort, we trained ourselves to stay in discomfort — out of devotion to those we care deeply about?

What if instead of distraction, we deepened into purpose?

This book is important, because in the distracted, anxiety-filled world we've created, we struggle to create anything of meaning, to do anything but follow our old habitual patterns. And we can sometimes feel helpless in the face of those old patterns and powerful distraction-laden environment.

This book is for anyone who:

- Wants to start a business that does good in the world but struggles with self-doubt and fears
- Wants to make a positive impact but struggles with feeling overwhelmed
- Wants to lead a team or organization but struggles with frustration and overwhelm
- Wants to create space for their meaningful work but feels pulled in a thousand directions, never sure they're doing the right thing
- Wants to feel a sense of purpose in their lives but feels constantly busy with the churn of daily tasks
- Wants to go deeper into mindfulness and develop a new relationship with themselves and everyone around them

If that's you, this book is for you. This is not an easy path, because it requires you to practice, over and over again.

It also requires you to take every struggle you have with the practice — from not doing it to feeling like you're doing it wrong — and *use that as your path*. Use the struggle as an opportunity to practice, as a way to open even more. In this way, every struggle becomes our teacher, and in fact helps us to deepen.

If you practice, I promise, things will shift. After a month, you'll see yourself procrastinating less. You'll be more mindful. After several months, your old patterns of avoidance will start to loosen. You'll be more open to the moment, more grateful. After six months, you'll start to see transformation. After a year, you'll be on a path to absolute transformation and deepening. If you practice.

This book is meant to be a short read, so that you can read it in a few days if you'd like. But while the first read might be short, the actual work will be a lifetime.

With this book, I'm issuing a powerful invitation to you: come with me on this journey, to dive deeply into your purpose, the habitual patterns that are getting in your way, and the incredible training that is contained in these pages.

Chapter 1: The Problem

We have to be honest with ourselves. We have to see our gut, our real shit, our most undesirable parts. We have to see that. That is the foundation of warriorship and the basis of conquering fear. We have to face our fear; we have to look at it, study it, work with it, and practice meditation with it.

~CHÖGYAM TRUNGPA

If our goal is to play video games and watch TV shows all day, or check social media and reply to messages all day, there is no problem. That's easy, and our minds are geared towards doing these comfortable distractions.

The problem comes when we decide we want to do something with purpose. We want to do meaningful work each day. We want to make an impact on the world. This is great! What's the problem, right?

Well, as we all know, it's not always so easy. We set ourselves to do some meaningful work, but we then feel doubts, fears, resistance. Then we start putting it off, avoiding, distracting, finding busywork, anything but this fearful thing. Then we start feeling bad about ourselves, doubting our ability to do it.

Sound familiar?

This works in three parts:

1. You decide to do some meaningful work -->
2. Which causes uncertainty to arise in you -->
3. Which causes you to run to a habitual pattern (procrastination, distraction, control, etc.)

And the habitual pattern usually leads to things piling up, you feeling bad about yourself, deadlines being missed, you trusting yourself less, health problems, relationship problems, and much more.

UNCERTAINTY IS THE ROOT

The root of all of this is **uncertainty**:

- I don't know if I can do it
- I don't know what others will think of me
- I don't know if I'm doing the right thing
- I don't know if I chose the right thing to do right now
- I don't know how to do this
- I don't know what the hell I'm doing
- I don't like any of this
- I don't know if I'll be OK
- I don't know if I'm good enough
- I don't know if I'm worthy of love

This uncertainty is absolutely normal. In fact, it makes complete sense: how can we ever be certain about anything? The world isn't certain, so we're going to feel uncertainty.

Uncertainty isn't the problem — in fact, it can be absolutely beautiful. The problem is that **we don't like the feeling of uncertainty**. Our minds can feel anxious because of uncertainty. It is like the ground being taken out from under our feet — what Pema Chodron calls "groundlessness." And so, without ground under our feet, we immediately and anxiously grasp around for some kind of ground, some kind of stability.

Our minds want stability, not groundlessness. And so we habitually seek stability: comfort, routine, certainty, control. **All of our unhelpful habitual patterns stem from this seeking of control, certainty and comfort when we feel uncertainty, groundlessness**.

THE GROUND OF HABITUAL PATTERNS

When we seek control and certainty, it results in habitual patterns:

- Procrastination
- Putting off healthy habits like exercise, flossing, meditation
- Trying to control a situation by planning, lists, systems, routines
- Grasping anxiously for control and feeling anxiety
- Lashing out at others in frustration and anger
- Perfectionism
- Complaining, seeing things as burden or chore
- Seeking distractions when you're overwhelmed
- Staying in busywork instead of focus
- Trying to exit when it's uncomfortable

- Judging, feeling superior
- Taking on too much, wanting to do everything
- Constantly worrying about missing out
- Ignoring a problem
- Avoiding playing a bigger game
- Eating comfort foods, watching TV, playing games
- Smoking, biting nails, constant porn

And so on — you get the picture. Anything where you're seeking control, avoiding, putting things off, seeking comfort. Anything where you're seeking ground to avoid the feeling of groundlessness.

These are not helpful habitual patterns. They make everything more difficult. They make us unhealthy. They stop us from doing our meaningful work, or if we do manage to do the work, stop us from enjoying it.

We could try to solve this by getting rid of all uncertainty in our world — and some people try this, by getting control of everything, having systems and routines and checklists. These are not bad things, and can even be helpful. But in the end, they don't give us certainty.

We could just love ourselves despite all of our unhelpful habitual patterns, accept that this is how we are. And this is helpful, developing a loving attitude toward ourselves. But it's only part of the solution — in the end, the unhelpful patterns will still destroy efforts for a healthy life and meaningful work and relationships.

The path is to train ourselves out of the habitual patterns. To learn to face the uncertainty, face the feelings of fear and stress and anxiety that come up when we feel uncertainty, and even face the urge to run to our old patterns.

The path is to train to fearlessly be with the uncertainty, and then learn to shift the patterns as we open up to the groundlessness of every moment. This is the path of this book.

Chapter 2: The Opportunity

*If we learn to open our hearts, anyone,
including the people who drive us crazy, can be our teacher.*

~PEMA CHÖDRÖN

So the problem is that our minds don't like the uncertainty that's everpresent in our lives, and we run to habitual patterns to grasp for ground in a groundless world. This is a problem, but it's just as much an opportunity.

The opportunity is to **use our struggles to do meaningful work as our training ground**. If we procrastinate on writing, this is our training ground. This is exactly where we need to practice.

The opportunity is to use our unhelpful habitual patterns to open us up instead of continuing to shut us down. And by using the habitual patterns to train, we can then get good at being in uncertainty so we don't need to run anymore. In fact, we can learn to relax in the middle of uncertainty, open up in possibility, fall in love with the groundlessness. Then push deeper into purpose.

The opportunity is to not need to run anymore, because we are no longer afraid of our feelings of fear, anxiety, stress, loneliness, frustration, anger, resistance, closing.

How do we do this? Well, we start by seeing the opportunity in every struggle:

- When we say we're going to meditate but put it off, we can beat ourselves up. Then we can see the opportunity to work with our urge to put off the meditation, as well as work with the tendency to beat ourselves up.
- When we fight with our partner because they criticized us, we can see the opportunity to open up our hearts to them in the middle of the stress of feeling criticized. We can see the opportunity to use their pain as a path to connection and intimacy with them.
- When we feel bad about ourselves for not exercising or eating healthy, and we dislike the way our bodies look … we can see the opportunity to become closer to the pain of not liking ourselves (or parts of ourselves), to shift our relationship to ourselves, and to move closer to loving acts like exercise and healthy food.

Every single struggle becomes our teacher, and our practice ground. Every struggle is an opportunity to practice with groundlessness, with fear and anxiety. Every struggle is an opportunity to shift our patterns, shift our relationship with our experience, shift into openness.

We can train ourselves to see the opportunity in the struggle, in the habitual patterns, in the fears and failures. This is what the training is about.

Chapter 3: The Training

We are always in transition.
If you can just relax with that, you'll have no problem.

~CHÖGYAM TRUNGPA

There are an infinite amount of ways to train with all of this, because every struggle is an opportunity to practice. But in this book, we're going to use our meaningful work as the training ground.

Why use meaningful work instead of health habits like exercise, smoking or meditation, or organization habits like decluttering and finances, or relationship struggles? A number of reasons:

- If we have meaningful work we'd like to do in the world, and shift our patterns around that work, we can have a positive impact on the world.
- Using our meaningful work as the training ground gets us good at the training but also at the meaningful work.
- It can be a more stable training ground to do a certain kind of work every morning (for example) rather than trying to work with the random times you have relationship problems, or the many times you have to deal with the urge to eat unhealthy comfort foods.

- If we get good at training in the uncertainty of meaningful work, it easily translates into the other areas of our lives.

So let's say your meaningful work is writing a book or a blog. Great! Your writing is your training ground. Here's how that training might look:

1. You decide you want to write a book. You decide that if you sit down and write every day for 30 minutes, you'll make great progress in the book. So you set for yourself the daily practice of "write for 30 minutes every day at 7am."
2. You pick the time, set up a reminder, pick a place, and get your writing tools set up, and make sure there are no distractions from writing come 7am (an Internet blocker is a good idea, for example).
3. When the time comes to write, you sit down to write. But you're feeling doubt and fear, so you go to your favorite websites instead! This is your habitual pattern coming up. After three days of doing that, you can see your habitual pattern very clearly. Maybe you knew it before, but because you set this writing as a training session for yourself, it becomes very clear now.
4. Now when it's time to sit down and write, you resolve to not run to your favorite websites … but instead to sit there and practice with the fears and doubts that are coming up. You sit and face them, meditate on them (more on this in upcoming chapters), and open up to them. Maybe you get no writing done today, but you practiced with the fears and didn't allow yourself to run to your habitual pattern.

5. You do this for several days, and get good at practicing with the fears. Then you actually do some writing! For several days, you actually get a decent amount of writing done.
6. You do a weekly review and solidify your learning, deepening your intentions.
7. Then other patterns come up — rationalizations, resistance, getting your email done, organizing your finances. You practice with these as well. Eventually, with practice and weekly reviews, you get really good at practicing with whatever comes up and not indulging in the urge to run to the ground of your habitual patterns.

As you can see, the writing is not really the point — **it's the training ground that will induce uncertainty and habitual patterns**. The writing will get done, but even on the days when you don't write, you are still practicing with the uncertainty.

That's what the training looks like. The training ground is the meaningful work, but the training is practicing with the fears and patterns. With training like this over weeks and months, you'll start to see a shift in your habitual patterns, an opening where there was closing.

Chapter 4: The Shift

Stop acting so small.
You are the universe in ecstatic motion.

~RUMI

The shift that you can see in your old patterns is not theoretical. I've been training in this myself for a decade and have seen huge shifts, and have been coaching people 1-on-1 and in my Fearless Training Program for more than a year, and have seen some amazing shifts from people who train in this method wholeheartedly.

For myself, the shifts have really surprised me:

- I am more focused than ever before, and creating more content in several programs, coaching six people at a time, writing for my blog and creating ebooks and video courses
- I feel more connected to my deeper purpose than I have in my entire life, and it is incredibly gratifying
- While I am not free of bad habits, I'm now able to change old habits more easily than anytime before now
- I can see my patterns in my relationships (marriage, kids, friends, other loved ones) and see how they are

not helpful … and while these have taken longer to shift, I am now more open-hearted, more loving, more grateful for these people in my life than ever before

These are just some of the shifts, but they have had a huge impact on my life and my ability to do my meaningful work.

I'll share a few more examples from others:

- Jan has trained wholeheartedly in the Fearless program and says, "I'm finally facing the fear, insecurity, and resistance that I have avoided looking at all my life." And I can personally testify that it is very visible — she is creating a course that she struggled with creating, she's developing confidence in herself, and deepening her spiritual path in a very courageous way.
- Nicola said that the training is helping her take her business to a new level. She says, "Learning to sit with uncertainty rather than "organise it away" is exactly what I need to push myself as an entrepreneur. Rather than keeping busy with all the easy stuff, I'm now finding that I'm more willing and able to focus on the scary stuff that matters."
- Loic is someone who is deeply mindful and thoughtful, and his practice has been inspiring. He says, "This training has allowed me to face aspects of my life that I had almost given up on and turn the rocks that I did not dare touch. Thanks to this program, and after 20 years of trying, I have finally anchored an uplifting morning routine. More notably, I am now overcoming a writing phobia and on course to launching my first book."

These are just a few examples, but there are dozens and dozens of them — people who have been creating businesses, writing books, starting blogs, practicing music in public, doing public speaking, changing their health, meditating, and in general just creating powerful shifts in their lives.

Honestly, it has blown me away and humbled me. Their wholehearted efforts and beautiful practice have been inspiring. The shifts they've seen have almost seemed effortless after the deliberate practice they'd been putting in.

This training has opened me, and has opened many others. The benefits have been innumerable, but perhaps some of the most fundamental benefits have been less noticeable:

- A willingness to face fears and uncertainty, to be with our experience
- A shift in our relationship with ourselves, to something kinder, gentler, more friendly
- An increase in mindfulness throughout the day
- Increased trust in ourselves to stay with something even when it gets difficult, to show up when we say we're going to show up
- A deeper sense of fulfillment in general

These benefits haven't come to every single person, but I've seen it many times. The more sincere the practice, the more these benefits show up. Not all at once, not immediately, but with time and practice. It has been breathtaking.

Chapter 5: Depth of Purpose

> *You don't have to find your mission, you need to relax in the moment to discover it. You say, "I don't know, so I will sit upright as open awareness until I know." You don't distract yourself with beaches, playmates, and oceans, searching for things that are merely delicious. Finding your purpose is fully sinking into the present moment and letting reality manifest through you as a gift to all.*
>
> ~DAVID DEIDA

Before we start the training, it's important to deliberate on your deep purpose. What meaningful work will be your training ground, and why is this something you care deeply about?

As we contemplate deep purpose, let's talk about two different parts of our journey:

1. You are still seeking your purpose.
2. You have some kind of purpose but don't feel connected to it.

Each becomes an area for exploration.

DELIBERATE ON YOUR PURPOSE

If you're still seeking your purpose, or not quite sure yet, you're in an area of uncertainty. What is your mind trying to do in reaction to the groundlessness of not knowing your purpose? How is it trying to run or shut down?

Instead of indulging in that pattern, turn and face the uncertainty. And explore by giving it some space for deliberation.

Some ways to explore:

- **Give yourself space to deliberate and explore**. That means getting away from your usual distractions and busyness, to somewhere you have some stillness, silence, space. Perhaps go out in nature. Give yourself a day, two days, a week. Repeat this as often as needed until you have at least a small degree of clarity.
- **Listen, in silence**. Let yourself find silence, away from devices, away from noise, so that you can sit in stillness and silence and just listen. Notice what you feel. It won't be obvious what it means at first, but after listening for awhile, you'll notice what you yearn for. What gives you joy, a sense of adventure, a sense of play. What creates pain and the wish to salve that pain. What you are afraid of, what fills you with doubt, what makes you want to run.
- **In this silence, ask what you're being called to do**. From a place of stillness and consciousness, ask yourself what life is calling you to do. See what answer comes up. It might be something relatively small

("help my mom today"), but it might be more ("I need to work with children who are struggling").
- **Reflect on your journey**. What have you gone through? What struggles have you faced? What have you climbed out of? How have you grown and learned? What pain have you felt that's taught you something? Now ask, "Who else struggles with this, has this pain, needs the lessons I've been learning, needs to go on a similar journey?"
- **Connect your heart to those who you care about**. Think about other people you care about — not just friends and loved ones, but people who you serve, people who you feel connected to, people you feel compassion for. As you sit in meditation, send them compassion. "May they find peace. May there be an end to their pain." Repeat it, with a compassionate feeling in your heart, over and over, as you visualize these people. Feel your heart connect to theirs. Ask how you can serve them.
- **Have a conversation with others, and listen**. Ask people who know you to reflect back to you what you care about, who you care about. What makes you joyful, what you are passionate about. What you'd be good at, what you've learned in the last few years. What they can see you doing. Talk to as many people as you can, especially people who know you and who you trust. Listen. Write down their ideas.
- **Make a list of everything you do right now**. Which activities give you meaning and fulfillment? Which don't?
- **Make a list of things you've done in the past that have given you meaning**. Are there any connections

between them? Any connections to the ones on your current list?
- **Open to suffering in your life**. Things become more meaningful when you've been through suffering — it's not something to be avoided, but something to work with, something to grow with, a path to deeper meaning. Think about the most meaningful experiences in your life — they probably involved other people, and they probably involved some kind of suffering.

These won't necessarily give you absolute clarity, but you will get more clarity doing these things than if you don't.

But there's an important point to understand: you get clarity from action. Many people want to get clarity of purpose before they act. But actually, you have to act before you can truly get clarity. Pick a purpose that feels "kind of" right, but even if you don't feel very clear, take action. Again and again. And you'll get the clarity you'll need.

To do that, move to the next exploration below.

CONNECTING TO YOUR PURPOSE

Once you have a slight amount of clarity (you don't have to have absolute clarity), the exploration is about connecting to your purpose on a regular basis.

It can be a challenge to connect to purpose throughout the course of the day, because we get caught up in busyness and forget the deeper purpose that is our mission. Without that connection, the tasks don't seem meaningful.

Some ways to explore connecting to that purpose:

1. **Meditate on the purpose to connect to those you care about**. At the start of your day, you might sit for a few minutes and meditate on who you care deeply about. Meditate on why you care about helping them. Meditate on their hearts, and the struggle they're going through (more on this in the next chapter). Let this connect you to them, and you will dive into your tasks from a deeper place.
2. **Keep your purpose front of mind**. Throughout the day, take a moment to reflect on your purpose. How are you living it? How can you go deeper or expand with it? What one or two things can you do today to serve that purpose?
3. **Set an intention with each task**. If you're going to write an article, record a video, clean a church floor, see a patient … start that activity by setting an intention to serve the people you care deeply about with love, mindfulness, devotion, or whatever you want to bring to that activity. It helps to set the intention, because the activity becomes filled with purpose, instead of something not very meaningful.
4. **Have regular reviews**. I've found that it's one thing to have an intention, but it's another to actually live it. We forget, we get distracted, we fall into habitual patterns. To get us back on track, it really helps to have regular reviews. For example: have a 5-minute review at the end of the day — how did you do today? How can you get

better? Maybe write 1-2 sentences in a journal. Or just reflect on it. Do the same each week: plan out your week on Sundays (for example), but also review your past week. How can you adjust for the upcoming week? And each month, and each year. Put these on your calendar and don't skip it when the review date comes up!

5. **Have people hold your purpose in their hearts**. Find at least 1-2 other people (and ideally more) who will hold your purpose in their hearts. That means: you tell them about it, they care about you and what you're doing, and they'll ask you about it, maybe support your mission in some way. They'll challenge you if they feel you're not doing everything you can or living your best life. They'll share their mission with you. They'll be on the journey with you, because no one fulfills their deepest purpose alone.

6. **Connect to your fulfillment**. Reflect on the meaning you get from fulfilling your purpose. Don't just go through the motions — feel it, deeply. Feel the love you're offering (and receiving) as you push into this purpose. See the good you're doing for others. Live your life as love.

This is an exploration, not a step-by-step process to follow. Let yourself explore ways to connect to your purpose, play with it, find what helps you to connect the most to what you care most deeply about.

Chapter 6: The Deeper Love

*The essence of warriorship, or the essence of human bravery,
is refusing to give up on anyone or anything.*

~CHÖGYAM TRUNGPA

In the last chapter, I touched on the people you care about deeply. This is worth going into a bit more, as the love you feel for these people will be what holds you in this training.

This groundlessness training will get uncomfortable — to shift out of our old habitual patterns, we have to be willing to experience discomfort. The unwillingness to experience discomfort is how we created those habitual patterns in the first place. When we hold ourselves in the discomfort of not running to the patterns, then the patterns start to shift. Then we become free of them.

So when things get uncomfortable, what will stop us from running? **We have to have a deeper reason we're doing this, because "it sounds like a nice idea" won't cut it when our patterns of wanting to shut down or run start to kick in**.

The two things that will hold us in the discomfort of the training:

1. Having people who we care about deeply (our clients, community, team, patients, students), and connecting to the love we feel for them; and
2. Having a small group of people who we're practicing with who will hold us to our intentions

We'll talk about the second item in the next chapter ("The Container"), but it's important to start with the first item — the people we care about deeply. They are the reasons you're doing this training in the first place, they're the reason your meaningful work is meaningful. You are doing the work to serve them, out of love.

Let's look at a few scenarios to illustrate this idea:

- You are starting a non-profit to serve abused women and children. You aren't doing it for money, prestige, ego — you're doing it because you care about the people who would be helped by this service. You have love in your heart for them, and deep compassion for their pain. They make your work meaningful, and make the training in uncertainty worth the discomfort.
- You are a therapist who is writing a book about being kind to yourself. You are writing it after having seen so many people who are harsh toward themselves, who beat themselves up for small mistakes, who have anxiety because they think they've wrecked everything. You know them because in many ways you *are* them. You've learned the healing power of being kind to yourself, and want to share that with them. Your love for them is why you're writing this book.

- You're creating a startup to bring mindfulness to people's everyday lives. Not because "it would be nice" but because you've seen the transformative power of mindfulness in your own life, and in the lives of many others. You know that people need this, because you see how being caught up in their thoughts causes them to suffer. You care about them greatly, and want only to help. Your love for them drives you through the struggles of running a startup, and the discomfort of this training.

I could give a few dozen more examples: teachers who care about their students, bloggers who write for those like them who think they're alone, people who have ADHD who want to help others like them, parents of autistic children who want to help other parents like them, a musician who knows their music will bring love to those who need it.

No matter what you do or who you are, your work will be more meaningful if you have people you are serving out of love.

Who are they? What are they going through? What struggles do they have that you can help with? What struggles have you had that you've learned from, that others might be going through?

Meditate on these people, visualizing them in their struggles, feeling their pain. Send out a compassionate wish, from the tender place in your heart where you feel love, a compassionate wish for their pain to end. Let this compassionate wish connect your tender heart to theirs.

And connect to this love for them, and their pain, on a daily basis. To drive your meaningful work, and your training in groundlessness.

WHAT MAKES THE DISCOMFORT WORTH IT

The training, as I've said, will be uncomfortable. You'll be asked to stay in the discomfort instead of running, instead of indulging in your old patterns of shutting down, exiting, running, complaining, rationalizing, avoiding.

Why put yourself through discomfort? What makes it worth it?

Your love for the people you care about and serve. That makes it worth it.

When you're in the middle of discomfort, remind yourself that your love for these people is so much bigger than your discomfort. Your discomfort becomes a small matter when you consider the vastness of your love for them.

Their hearts are more important than a little discomfort. Their hearts are worth the focus the training will require, the constant effort to shift your patterns. They are worth your growth.

This training, then, becomes bigger than your self-concern. And that is a massive shift for most of us.

Chapter 7: The Container

Set your life on fire.
Seek those who fan your flames.

~RUMI

Before we dive into the actual training, it's important to set up structure. I call this the "container" for your training — it's the space where you practice, that holds you safely in the training. The environment that you consciously set up so that you'll be able to deepen the training, so that you won't run, so that you're more likely to see an actual shift.

You can see practice containers in a lot of conscious practices — when a yoga teacher sets up a room so that students can feel safe and be completely immersed in their practice, when a coach or therapist creates agreements so that the client feels safe and can open up and do deep work, when a Zendo creates a quiet and meditative physical environment and a set of rules of conduct so that everyone in the meditation hall can go deep into their practice.

A good practice container might have some of these elements:

- **Safety**: You can't relax into the practice if you don't feel physically safe, or safe to open up, share, go deep.

A good container will consider how to make the practitioner feel safe enough to practice deeply.

- **Physical environment**: Beyond safety, your physical environment affects how you feel, how you might be mindful or relax, how you might move about in the space. Is there music, incense, an altar, posters, photos, plants, a pond, an ocean, candles, lights, darkness, stillness, silence, pillows, yoga mats, writing implements, a beanbag? Are the windows closed, the door open to the outside world? How do all of these things affect the practice?
- **Agreements**: You might set up agreements between the people practicing, or between coach and client, or just with yourself. Agreements might include things like confidentiality, be on time, no talking, complete and brutal honesty, respect others, no judgments, take care of yourself, and so on. How does each agreement affect the practice?
- **Invite openness & curiosity**: What is the invitation in the container? Does it invite the person to explore with openness, to be curious, to create intimacy or possibility? The invitation can be for many other things as well, but it's worth asking what the invitation is and how that will affect the practice.
- **Intentions to start, gratitude to close**: How will the practice start and end? It might start with a bow, a prayer, an invitation, a meditation. One possibility is starting by consciously setting your intentions for the practice session, and ending by bowing in gratitude for how you showed up.

This isn't a definitive list of what to consider as you set up a practice container. Instead, they're examples of things to consider as you set up a practice.

THE CONTAINER FOR OUR TRAINING

So how are we going to set up our uncertainty training? Here's the structure I recommend and train with myself:

1. **Pick meaningful work to focus on, to serve people you care about**. Let's say you want to write a book to help people become more vulnerable, or create a video course for those who struggle with reading. You have people in your heart who you care about, and are doing the meaningful work for them.
2. **Set a goal for the month, with a review at the end of the month**. If you're writing a book, set a goal for this month to write 4 chapters (or 8 chapters, or whatever you think is doable). If you're creating an app, set a goal to write a certain amount of code. Same thing for videos, blogging, getting funding, talking to prospective clients. The goal isn't set in stone, but something to aim for. Have a reminder to do a review for how you did at the end of the month.
3. **Choose something you can do every day, as a practice**. Now convert the monthly goal into a daily activity. Write every day for 30 minutes. Record or edit a video each day. Call 3 potential clients. This activity isn't the training itself, it's the training ground, to see what uncertainty comes up. If the activity doesn't give you uncertainty, you're playing too small a game — be bolder and step up the game.

4. **Have a group of people holding your intention (your accountability crew), and check in with them weekly**. It's possible to do this training without other people, but I've found that most people won't sustain the training for very long on their own. I believe it should be mandatory to have at least several other people who you use to hold yourself accountable — I call them your "accountability crew." Ideally, it's other people doing the training — for this, I recommend my Fearless Training Program. The key is to share your intentions with them, let them hold those intentions in their hearts, and then feel solidly committed to them. And check in every week on a certain day (Monday, for example) — report how you did with your intentions, what victories you had, what struggles, what you learned. What pattern is showing up? What have you seen shift? Then share your intentions for the coming week. In this way, you'll learn and be able to adjust your training.
5. **Pick a time and place, and carefully consider your physical environment**. If you are going to write, when and where are you going to write? Where will you be when you call potential clients or record videos? Consider how the physical environment will affect the training — do you want to shut off the Internet, play music, have tea, clear the space, turn off your phone? Pick a time and try to do the training every day at that time. If something comes up to interfere with doing it at that time, consciously pick another time to do it. But don't give in to your rationalizations.
6. **Do your meaningful work as your training, and practice with the uncertainty that comes up**. At the

time and place you set for your training, do the task you set for yourself. If you feel like putting it off, notice what you have an urge to do instead (your pattern). Instead of indulging in the pattern, train with the feeling of uncertainty that comes up. (More on the specifics of this training in the next chapter.) Maybe you are doing it but feel like switching. Notice this, practice with the uncertainty. Maybe you're doing it but not liking it, complaining about it, dreading it. Notice this and practice.

7. **Make note of the habitual patterns that come up, or have others call them out for you**. As you attempt to do your meaningful work in each practice session, you'll start to notice your old patterns arising. That's good news! Now you can get clear on the patterns. If you don't see the patterns, talk to someone else about it, let them ask you questions, and then let them honestly and lovingly call out the patterns. More on this in a later chapter on calling out patterns.

8. **Shift your pattern by repeatedly staying in the uncertainty instead of running**. As you become clear on your pattern, you'll see it more and more clearly. You'll be aware when you have the urge to indulge in the pattern. Instead, stay in the uncertainty, stay in the discomfort of not running, and after continued training in this, you will shift the pattern. More on shifting the pattern in a later chapter.

9. **Acknowledge & note your victories**. It's important to see the progress you've made — it helps to encourage you, reinforce the good patterns, and solidify your learning. So each week, note the small and large victories you've had. These are worth

celebrating! Let yourself feel good about them, and acknowledge your wholehearted efforts (even if they're not quite what you'd hoped to do). At the end of each month, look back on your weekly check-ins and list your victories for the month. After a few months, list all your victories in one place. These shifts are worth noting.

This is the structure of the training. We'll dive deeper into individual elements in coming chapters, but this is the container I highly recommend that you create for your training. If you do, you're setting yourself up for success and are more likely to see major shifts.

Chapter 8: The Training Session & the Fearless Practice

Run from what's comfortable.
Forget safety.
Live where you fear to live.

~RUMI

You're sitting down to do your training session, with the piece of meaningful work you've set for yourself. Maybe it's to write a chapter in your book (as an example). How do you do the actual training? What does a training session look like?

Taking the book writing as an example … the training session might start by clearing your physical space, setting up some relaxing music, turning off the Internet and your phone, closing all apps but your writing app, brewing a cup of tea, and reviewing your notes. You're setting up your practice space.

Contemplate the people you care about, the people you're serving by doing this meaningful work. Connect to their hearts. Set your intention for this session: "To serve the people I care about by writing a chapter to help them."

Now you are ready to start writing. You have them in your heart as you start. You set a timer for 20 minutes (for example).

Then you feel your urge to run to your habitual pattern (checking email or social media, doing busywork, etc.) … and you notice the urge.

You practice with this urge to run using the Fearless training practice (see next section).

Maybe you're able to do some writing. Then after a bit, your uncertainty comes up and you notice the urge to switch to something else. You practice again, using the Fearless training practice below.

Your timer goes off, and you bow silently in gratitude for the training you've done.

That's what a training session might look like. Of course, the specifics will vary depending on the kind of meaningful work you're doing, and the setup you've created for your training. But in general, that's how it works. It can be messier than that, but you can see the basic way it goes.

Let's look at how to practice with the fear and uncertainty and the urge to run to your patterns. I call it the basic Fearless practice.

THE BASIC FEARLESS PRACTICE

By "basic" I mean fundamental. This Fearless practice is how you'll work with whatever comes up, or at least it will be how you start to work with it. It will be so fundamental that you will get good at it, and in doing so, you'll get good at being in groundlessness.

The basic Fearless practice is to be fully with whatever feelings come up when you're in uncertainty (and you're always in uncertainty).

Here's how it looks:

1. **You feel fear, uncertainty, discomfort, or the urge to run.** This is where it starts. You normally don't even notice that you're feeling it, you just run to your habitual pattern. So after a while, you notice that you're feeling it because you just switched from writing to looking at social media. Then you notice because you notice the *urge* to switch to social media (before you actually switch). But some feeling of groundlessness has come up, and your mind doesn't like it. It might come up with a narrative about it, rationalizations, or just an urge to run.
2. **Instead of running, you turn towards the physical feeling of uncertainty.** Let's say you're feeling anxiety about a task, or about the overwhelming amount of tasks you have on your plate. You might have a narrative (or "story") in your head about it, "This is too much, I can't do it all, I don't have enough time, this is too hard, I need to find a way to get it all done,

I don't know what to do, maybe I should look at my phone instead!" This is your narrative, but what you need to turn toward is the physical sensation of the anxiety or feeling of overwhelm that's in your body. It might be in your chest, your stomach, your throat, or somewhere else. See if you can locate it in your body. You can try it right now, scanning your body for any sensations of uncertainty (which might feel like anxiety, frustration, fear, resistance, anger, sadness, pain, discomfort, etc.).

3. **Stay with the physical sensations, with curiosity**. It's important to not judge these sensations, not label them as "bad" or "unpleasant," but instead to just observe. Just see what you can notice about them. Can you be curious about this sensation? Where is it located, what shape does it take, does it have a temperature, color, texture? Does it change? Does it move? Is it solid, liquid, hollow, heavy, radiant? Being curious allows us to be more open with this sensation.

4. **Stay with the sensation, with gentleness and friendliness**. Already, we've been more open and more present with the sensations of uncertainty than most people ever do. Let's continue that courageousness by staying with it for a little longer. Can you continue to bring curiosity in noticing what you can about the sensation? Can you bring an attitude of gentleness and warm friendliness toward the sensation? The same kind of warm friendliness we bring to being with a friend — that's what we're aiming for with this sensation of uncertainty. We're transforming our relationship with our feelings and with uncertainty.

5. **Bring welcoming, even gratitude**. All of these ways of working with the sensation of uncertainty and our feelings are ways to make us more open. Another thing to try is welcoming the sensation, as you might welcome a good friend into your home. We're welcoming the sensation into our experience. Yet another thing to try is gratitude — can you be grateful for this sensation of groundlessness? It's a sign that you're alive, that you have a body, that you're training, that you're doing something meaningful that you're being courageous. A feeling of gratitude can open us nicely.

Play with these ways of being with the groundlessness. There's no single way to practice, but it's about fearlessly being with the pain, discomfort, fear, difficulty, resistance, frustration, overwhelm, anxiety. Fearlessly being with whatever comes up, in a way that is gentle, friendly, curious, open. This transforms our relationship to our feelings, to our experience. It helps us to become more comfortable with our discomfort, with groundlessness.

With practice, we can learn to relax into the groundlessness.

This is the basic Fearless practice. Practice it at least once a day, during the training session, but also anytime you notice uncertainty or one of the emotions mentioned above that come with uncertainty.

Chapter 9: Calling Out Patterns

When we know something and rest in that knowing we limit our vision. We will only see what our knowing will allow us to see.

~ZOKETSU NORMAN FISCHER

Once you set yourself to do your meaningful work in daily practice sessions, the patterns should start to show themselves. You'll find ways to put off starting, or switch after you start, or complain about the work and be unhappy about it.

When you notice yourself doing any of these things, pay close attention to what you run to. What is your mind trying to do to avoid the feeling of groundlessness and seek ground?

For example, you might be doing one of these things:

- Delaying starting (procrastinating) by going to busywork or your favorite distractions
- Starting then switching to distractions
- Doing the task but complaining about it, seeing it as a chore or burden
- Wanting to end the task because it's difficult, uncomfortable, painful - quitting early or really wanting to get to the end
- Rushing through the task

- Feeling overwhelmed, then going to distractions
- Breaking the chain of a habit or training program, then not starting again (or delaying re-starting)
- Beating yourself up, judging yourself, thinking you're doing things wrong
- Perfectionism — especially not doing something because conditions are not perfect. It has to be perfect, or it doesn't happen at all
- Avoiding tackling something because you doubt yourself or it's uncomfortable
- Complaining about other people, due to your own insecurities
- Comparing yourself to other people (feeling worse than them, feeling superior)
- Trying to control things so you don't have to feel uncertainty
- Shutting down your heart so you don't have to feel the other person's anger
- Getting stuck in a narrative about how you're not good enough
- Avoiding doing anything too big, playing a smaller game
- Doing everything yourself instead of delegating (not wanting to lose control)
- Ignoring a problem, pretending it doesn't affect you or others in your life
- Give up in frustration, or close your heart after frustration
- Being resentful
- Wanting to do everything, wanting to get everything done
- Working on smaller tasks

You might be doing a combination of some of these, or maybe you have a different pattern than anything listed here.

Notice what's going on, and write it down. This is one of your patterns. Now that you know it, you can start to see it clearly, and then start to shift it. Be as honest with yourself as possible, rather than believing your rationalizations.

USING OTHERS TO CALL OUT PATTERNS

Often, we can't see the pattern ourselves. We see that we're struggling, but we don't see what's going on. This is when we need others to call out the patterns for us.

This is the typical way it goes when someone can't see their own pattern:

- They tell their accountability group that they're going to do something every day (record a video, for example)
- Then they don't do it
- Then they give the group a handful of reasons why they couldn't do it this past week
- This repeats for awhile, and then they rationalize giving up that goal and trying something else

This has happened to all of us, except many times we do it without the accountability group, so we don't need to report that we've failed, we just keep it to ourselves and believe our rationalizations.

We need to find people who don't believe our rationalizations, but can look at what's going on and spot the pattern, then reflect the pattern back to us in a non-judgmental way. This is what the small teams are for in my Fearless Training Program — they're asked to call out the patterns of their teammates.

Here's how you can call out a pattern for someone else:

1. **Let the person tell you the struggle they're having with their training**. They haven't been doing it lately, they just can't start, they were doing well but got interrupted and can't start again. They should give you all their reasons for the struggle.
2. **Ask some clarifying questions**. Dig around a little to try to find the pattern — what do they do instead of the training when it's time to train? What do they tell themselves? Why aren't they doing it? What's getting in the way? How does that feel?
3. **When you think you see a pattern, pause and ask permission to share it with them**. Only ask as many questions as needed to see the pattern you think is going on. Most likely: They're avoiding doing it because it's scary or uncomfortable, and they're rationalizing why it's OK. And maybe beating themselves up too. When you see the pattern, ask for permission to reflect back to them what you see. Asking for permission allows them to decide if they're ready.
4. **When they give permission, you should share with love and without judgement, while they try to drop defensiveness**. Share the pattern you see with honesty, but from a place of compassion — it's likely

you have had (or still have) the same pattern, which is how you can spot it. Let it come from a place of love, but without holding back. In turn, they should try to drop any defensiveness, and receive your feedback as a gift — because that's what it is.

5. **They should assume you're right about the pattern**. They should thank you, but instead of showing why this is not their pattern, they should try to assume that you're right and that they just can't see it. It's possible you're not right, as we can't know for sure, but it's best if they assume you're right. Then they should go through the next week looking for evidence that you're right. Maybe you're wrong, and if they look for evidence but can't find it, then they can let go of your feedback. But if they find evidence, they should then work with that pattern.

Spotting someone else's pattern and giving them honest and loving feedback is a gift. We can't always do this for ourselves, so when someone else helps us, it's incredibly valuable.

Chapter 10: Hold the Pose to Shift the Patterns

When we find ourselves in a situation in which our buttons are being pushed, we can choose to repress or act out, or we can choose to practice.

~CHÖGYAM TRUNGPA

Now that you've gotten clear on your pattern(s), what can you do about it? Are we powerless against these old patterns that have hardened into habit since childhood? It can certainly seem that way.

But as I've said, in my own life and in the lives of others who have done this training, there have been massive shifts. Old habitual patterns don't go easily, but they aren't unshiftable.

The process of shifting the pattern goes something like this:

1. **Start to see the pattern more clearly**. At first, you might only spot it after the fact, which is why it's important to do a weekly review, so you can look back and see the pattern. But then you might notice it after you've been procrastinating for a few minutes (or hours). And soon you can see it just as it's happening,

or when the urge to go to the pattern arises. Become clear on when it's happening by spotting it as soon as you can.

2. **Be gentle with yourself, but face the urge fearlessly**. There is no need to beat yourself up because you've been indulging in the pattern — it's just an old habit, not anything to do with whether you're a good person (you are) or have self-worth (you do, no matter what you do). Instead, be gentle with yourself and your patterns. But that said, face the urge using the basic Fearless practice of turning toward the sensation of the urge. You'll find that it's exactly the same as fear, uncertainty, frustration — they're all just sensations in the body. Not a big deal, you've practiced with sensations before. Just feel the sensation of the urge to go to your pattern.

3. **Instead of indulging the urge, hold the pose**. The idea is to stay in the discomfort of not running to the pattern for a little while. Imagine yourself holding a yoga pose, but then getting shaky and wanting to get out of the pose. Instead of exiting, you **hold the pose** and stay in the discomfort. This is your edge, and you stay at the edge, at least for a little longer. One of my teachers, John Wineland, instructed us to, "Hold the fucking pose." We did, and we shifted. That's how change happens — you hold the pose, at your edge, in the discomfort. You do it again, and again, until you no longer need to run. Then you become free.

Discomfort, resistance, rationalizations will come up. Feel them, using the basic Fearless practice. Be gentle with them. Don't listen to the rationalizations but instead be with the sensation of pain that is causing the rationalizations. Feel the resistance and love it. Feel the discomfort and be fully with it.

With practice like this, holding the pose while you're at your edge, not listening to the rationalizations but being with the sensations of discomfort and uncertainty … things start to shift.

Soon, you are no longer beholden to the pattern. You begin to be comfortable with the urge but not a slave to it. You start to experience openness and freedom, instead of a small, closed-in sense of self-concern.

Your love for the people you care deeply about is bigger than your discomfort. Their hearts are worth holding the pose.

Chapter 11: Cultivating Fearlessness, Gentleness, Friendliness

Actual fearlessness is being intimate with your fear. What I've discovered is that I love this practice, because it's endless.

~ZENSHO SUSAN O'CONNELL
ZEN PRIEST

There's a way we can hold the pose and do this training that feels harsh, strict, disciplinarian. This is the kind of discipline that isn't helpful. It feels like we're forcing ourselves to do something terrible against our will, and harsh on ourselves when we're not "perfect" about it (perfect doesn't exist).

That kind of harshness isn't what we're trying to cultivate here. What we want to cultivate is gentleness and friendliness, and a fearlessness to be with the uncertainty and discomfort that we're facing. There's a huge difference between these approaches.

Let's take a look at each.

The harsh disciplinarian approach: I set a goal to code a video game every day, and when I come across discomfort getting started, I start getting mad at myself, telling myself not to wimp out. (This might be the voice of my dad, btw!) So I harshly push myself to do it, not approving of the parts of me that want to quit. I do it like this for a few days, but then I "wimp" out and don't do the coding. I feel terrible, and beat myself up about it, berating myself until I do it a few days later. I'm doing it but not happy, still feel bad about myself. This cycle repeats a few times until I quit, disgusted at myself.

This is basically the approach that most of us take, in some form or another. Let's look at a different way to go about it.

The gentle, friendly, fearless approach: I set the goal of coding everyday, and then immediately come up against discomfort. I pause and let myself feel the discomfort instead of running from it, and bring a gentle, friendly attitude toward the discomfort, bringing warmth into my heart as I curiously examine it. My wanting to run is also looked at with the same warmth and gentleness. None of it is bad or disgusting, just something happening in my body, not a judgment about me. I do the coding, practicing in the same way with whatever feelings come up as I code. A few days later, I give in to the urge to run, and don't code for the next 3 days. I look at this evasion as evidence of my habitual pattern, and again bring an attitude of gentleness and warm friendliness as I look at it. I gently start again, coming fearlessly close to whatever fears and discomfort come up. I'm much more likely to continue practicing this way, even if I struggle, because of this warmth and gentleness. More importantly, I'm transforming my relationship to my experience and myself.

As you can see, this is a much more helpful approach.

HOW TO CULTIVATE THESE QUALITIES

This approach isn't achieved overnight — it must be practiced. We can spend a month practicing this in a morning sitting meditation practice, being gentle and warm and friendly with our breath, with bodily sensations, with the thoughts that arise, with our attention as it jumps around.

This kind of practice informs our training, as we learn to take a less harsh approach. With this kind of gentle and friendly quality of our attention on whatever arises, we are more likely to become intimate with fear, uncertainty and discomfort.

Fearlessness is the willingness to come close to the fear and uncertainty, to be with it like you'd be with a close friend, a lover, someone you are intimate with in some way. It's being open to the feelings that arise, no matter what they are, fearlessly staying even when it's uncomfortable.

In this way, we are training ourselves to be fully present with our experience and the groundlessness of the experience. We can even find a way to love the experience, no matter what it's like. Normally we only love the "good" parts, and reject the "bad" parts, but this leads to clinging (to what we like) and aversion (to what we don't like), which only leads to suffering. Fearlessness is being with the experience no matter what, being open to it, falling in love with it.

Again, this takes practice. It takes a willingness to open when we want to close. To see the beauty in discomfort, when we just want to run from it. To come closer to it, open to it, see the groundlessness as gorgeous openness and not dangerous at all, but fresh and vast and freedom itself.

> *Sitting courageously at the center, we do not fight back or crumble in the face of pain. ... We honor and acknowledge all pain. We listen to all pain. The bodhisattva stays close to the pain without meddling or interfering. This is the path of Zen meditation.*
>
> ~TENSHIN REB ANDERSON

Chapter 12: Common Obstacles

We have to make a sustained effort,
again and again, to cultivate the positive aspects within us.

~THE DALAI LAMA

In this kind of training, there will be challenges that arise, as anything meaningful will call on you to grow in order to meet it. The good news is that these challenges are actually a part of the training, not something to be solved but actually the path itself. The struggles with this training *is* the training. The struggles are exactly what we need in order to grow.

So welcome every single obstacle as your teacher, your training ground, your companion on this journey.

That said, let's look at some common obstacles and how we might work with them.

1. **Too busy to do the training**: You're too busy, you don't have time for this training. Yep, we're all busy, and yet we somehow manage to do it! There is some truth to the busyness rationalization, which is what makes any rationalization powerful. But it's still a rationalization. Busyness is solved by focusing on fewer high-impact tasks, not by ignoring the high-

impact tasks so you can do the busywork. This training, and the meaningful work, are high-impact tasks. If you do them, it makes everything else better. You're too busy to afford *not* to do the training. Also: I don't buy the busyness excuse from anyone who watches video on Netflix or Youtube, plays games, reads websites, watches the news, or procrastinates in any way.

2. **Interrupted by travel, sickness, visitors, crisis**: Interruptions will happen, this is a part of life. Your first option, when you have an interruption, is to find a way to do the training anyway. Have visitors? Entertain them, show them around, but ask for 20 minutes to do your meaningful work (you can just call it "work" to them). Same thing when you're traveling — find a way. But sometimes this isn't an option, especially if you get sick or there's a crisis like an emergency or a death in the family. So your next option is to note that you got sidetracked, and simply set an intention to start up on the soonest possible date. Maybe that's next week Monday — set a reminder to start again. And simply start again, dropping any negative stories about yourself. If you have negative feelings, practice with them! Get close to any feelings of guilt, of overwhelm, of wanting to put off starting again. This is a practice opportunity.

3. **Missed the training & feeling discouraged**: You missed a few days after a good streak of practicing, and now you're feeling discouraged, guilty, wanting to quit. Maybe you missed a week. This feeling of discouragement is, of course, something to practice with. Do the basic Fearless practice of getting close to

the feeling of discouragement or guilt, being curious and open and gentle and warm. Let this moment of discouragement open you. Let it be the doorway into practice. And also ... find ways to encourage yourself. It absolutely matters whether we are encouraging or discouraging ourselves, so notice when you're discouraging yourself and shift it to encouragement however you can.

4. **Overwhelmed and so ignoring it all**: When we get overwhelmed, the logical step is to just start on the first step, and then take it one step at a time. Prioritize if you can. But of course, we're not logical beings — the common pattern is to feel overwhelmed and then not do anything, but instead ignore, avoid, distract, procrastinate. When you find this pattern, shout, "Aha!" This is a great discovery, because you've discovered one of your patterns, and you've been doing it for years. It's hurting you, as most of your patterns do. So do a dance of discovery, and then practice with it: be fearlessly intimate with the feeling of being overwhelmed, of wanting to quit or ignore. Then find the smallest next step you can do and get yourself moving. Movement begets movement. Start to shift this age-old pattern of yours.

5. **It's too hard, too hard, want to quit**: Yep, absolutely! This is uncomfortable stuff! And our old habits are all about running from discomfort as fast as we can. So ask yourself if you want to keep doing that — it will lead to the same results. You'll still be putting off your meaningful work, and nothing will change. You know how that feels — not great. You know how to ignore the not great feeling. But you can't really

ignore it, because actually you feel it. So why not try something new? Why not courageously face the discomfort, and learn to open up to uncertainty? Yes, it's hard, but it's not too hard, you can absolutely do it. I absolutely believe that. If an hour of writing is too hard for you, then do 30 minutes. Or 20 minutes. Or 10. If that's too hard, make it 2 minutes. There's no way you can't do 2 minutes. Start to shift this pattern, once and for all. You will love it once you've practiced for a bit.

6. **Feel that you're too tired to do a good or efficient job**: You can't always do the tasks you need to do when you have the most energy, so you need to accomplish things when your energy is lower … and so the brain can often rationalize that you're not going to do a good job, so don't do it at all. There is some truth to this, which makes it more powerful. However … if you look at it objectively (not when you're tired), it's not really true — you can do a decent job even when you're tired, and doing something is probably going to be better than doing nothing. If a task absolutely requires your best focus and energy, then schedule it for when you're at peak energy and let yourself do the less-important tasks when you're tired.

7. **Using tactics & strategy to overcome resistance and avoid uncertainty or discomfort, so you don't have to practice with the uncertainty or discomfort**: This is what most people try to do — find smart ways to set things up so that they don't have to face uncertainty and discomfort. For example, your day feels chaotic, so you try to structure it more rigidly so it doesn't feel chaotic. This is not necessarily

a bad idea — however, it doesn't really work. It might lessen the uncertainty, but you're just avoiding feeling discomfort ... this is the mind's usual tendency, and it's exactly what leads to our problems. In this training, we're actually trying to seek out the uncertainty and discomfort, to provoke it with our meaningful work, so that we can lean into it and train. By all means, use strategies in your normal life, but in the training itself, stay with the discomfort and practice with it. And if you spot it outside of the training, before you try to magic it away with techniques, actually stay with it and practice with it.

8. **Telling yourself that this is too small or insignificant to be worth the effort, and ask if it will even make a difference**: This is the mind rationalizing again! It's very good at trying to get out of the commitment, and in this case it's devaluing the task so that you don't have to do it. Don't let the mind talk you out of doing the task — make a commitment to your accountability crew and to yourself, and then just do it! You can always change it later if it's really not worth it, but get into the habit of just doing it. And of course, practice with the uncertainty that comes up, using the basic Fearless method.

9. **Wanting to use meditation or writing as the training instead of your meaningful work — writing can be a way of thinking about the work, right?** Meditation is OK to start with (perhaps for the first month), but it would be better to actually do your meaningful work. When people choose something other than their meaningful work, like meditation, they are usually putting off the meaningful work. I would rather they

move toward the thing they are resisting. And yes, Writing can be used for almost anything — but if you're writing to avoid calling clients or working on your design, I would say that should only be done a few times, then actually dive into the thing you're resisting.

10. **The tasks for your meaningful work are not things you can consistently do every day**: Sometimes different tasks have to be done in your meaningful work, or you do a task that's a one-off and not something you can do every day. That's OK! You can change the thing you're doing each day. Call clients one day, work on finances another, work on your website on the third day, write the other days, for example. **However** ... this can also be used as a way to avoid something. "I'll work on the website instead of the finances, it's still good!" (Even though you're avoiding the finances.) So instead, set what you're going to do at the beginning of the week and stick to that plan if at all possible. Change only as needed, and if necessary, ask others if the change is a good idea. Alternatively (only if you're good at this training, not as a beginner), you can ask yourself each day what you're resisting the most, and do that. The best Fearless practice is to work with what you're most resisting (unless that completely shuts you down, in which case it might be way too past your edge, but that's rarely the case).

11. **Signing up for too many programs or having too many practices to do**: Some people get very enthusiastic about signing up for things, because each program or practice offers a new solution, a promise to address a key uncertainty that you have. The key is

to 1) recognize that you're trying to solve your uncertainty by signing up for things or committing to new things, and 2) recognize that you're actually hurting yourself by being committed to too much. You can't do all of it, so it only increases your uncertainty. This is good news though! Now that you've given yourself so much uncertainty, see if you can practice with it before you make any changes. Stay with the feeling and see how many of the practices or programs you can actually do while practicing with the basic Fearless method. If it turns out you have way too much — not just the feeling that you have too much, but you physically can't do it all — then you need to make some changes and let go of commitments, and commit to less. Resist the temptation to solve your uncertainty by signing up for things.

There's no way to address all common problems, but you can start to get the idea of how to handle them by reading the answer above.

THE KEY IDEAS

Reading the answers above, a few key ideas stand out that we should keep in mind as other problems arise:

- **Don't believe the rationalizations**: This is the mind's way of getting out of the discomfort and uncertainty. If you use a certain rationalization a lot, this is one of your patterns. Notice the rationalization but don't let yourself give in to the urge to follow it.

Instead, practice with the discomfort and uncertainty that prompted the rationalization.

- **Practice with the difficulty**: As always, when any of these problems come up, see them as an opportunity to practice. Rationalizations come from uncertainty and discomfort — practice with these using the basic Fearless method. Every time you practice, you'll get better at it, and you can shift your patterns.
- **Set your intentions when you're not in the difficulty**: It's best to set your intentions for practice when you're not tired or trying to avoid the practice. Set it from your "best self" — when you are not coming from a place of fear or discomfort, but rather out of love for those you are serving. So set what you're going to do at the beginning of the week (after reviewing your past week) and then don't let yourself argue your way out of them, no negotiations allowed.
- **Review your problems & learn**: Each week, be sure to review how things are going. That's when these obstacles will make themselves clear. You'll be able to see what's been getting in the way of your training, and then think about it using the key ideas above this one, and learn from the obstacles. Grow. Get better at the training. Week after week, you'll get better at this, if you review and learn from the obstacles.

Keep coming back to this chapter if you struggle, and I believe it'll help you to work with whatever comes up.

Chapter 13: Adjusting the Training

To be fully alive, fully human, and completely awake is to be continually thrown out of the nest. To live fully is to be always in no-man's-land, to experience each moment as completely new and fresh. To live is to be willing to die over and over again.

~PEMA CHÖDRÖN

It often happens that the training structure from the Container chapter doesn't work, or that it works for awhile but then stops working. Or perhaps the meaningful work you chose for yourself is no longer relevant, no longer induces uncertainty, or is too intense for you to handle.

So what can we do? This is where the weekly check-in comes in — it allows you to assess how things are going, what obstacles you're facing, and what adjustments might be needed (if any). In this way, we have a flexible training system, not rigid structure but structure that supports change, learning, and constant improvement.

The idea for this comes from the Agile programming methods (and related methods like Scrum). In those methods, teams of programmers use regular check-ins and reviews to shift as needed, to iterate their work methods and the product they're creating as they learn each week, as they get feedback and see what problems emerge. In the same way, our Fearless training is flexible, able to adjust each week as we see what comes up, as we learn from the doing.

Each difficulty with the training, then, becomes a way for us to learn and adjust, to practice flexibility and resilience.

HOW TO ADJUST WITH WEEKLY REVIEWS

Every week, have a set day when you check-in with your accountability crew (whoever you decide that will be), and set up reminders so you don't forget. Commit to being as regular with these check-ins as possible, or everything will start to loosen and fall apart.

When you do your check-in, review your past week, answering these simple questions:

1. How did you do with your intentions in the past week? What victories or struggles did you have?
2. What did you learn? What adjustments need to be made?
3. What are your intentions for the coming week (including needed adjustments)?

This only takes 5-10 minutes, so don't let yourself indulge in the pattern of saying you're too busy, you're overwhelmed, you don't have time right now. Just do it, giving yourself just a little space to contemplate the questions.

Some adjustments you might need to make:

- **It's too easy and there was no uncertainty**: You might consider just staying the same for now. But after several weeks of no difficulties or uncertainty, up your game. Do it for longer, or find a harder version. For example, if practicing music is too easy, can you do it in public? If the business is going well and is too easy, can you decide to play a bigger game?
- **You didn't do it at all**: Look at what got in the way (rationalizations, scheduling) and see if you can fix that. Sometimes it helps to step up accountability — I've done fun things like promising to donate to my least favorite candidate if I didn't stick to my challenge, or asked a friend to promise to throw a pie in my face (and put a video of it on the Internet) if I didn't do what I promised to do. Deepen your commitment, and stop believing the rationalizations. Make it non-negotiable.
- **The time of day is wrong**: Maybe you planned to do your training at 6am but you can't get out of bed until 7am — so make your training at 7:30 am if possible. Maybe that's when the kids need to be readied for school and driven, so you have to reschedule for 10am or 7pm. You can find the time, but it might take a few adjustments.
- **The space where you train is wrong**: You decide to do your meaningful work in the living room, but people are always going through and interrupting you. So look for a quieter space, or find a coffee shop. There are lots of options that might work!
- **You absolutely hate the training**: You are doing it, but half-heartedly and with lots of aversion. First, celebrate and acknowledge that you're actually doing

the training! That's a big victory. Second, ask yourself if this is a pattern of yours — have you done other work where you ended up complaining about it? It's probably a habitual pattern of the mind to see things as burden, as a chore, as difficult and not worth it. See this as an opportunity to practice with this, and to shift to seeing the gift of the training, seeing the joy in it, finding ways to make it playful and fun (music might be helpful!). Find gratitude in the doing.

These are only a few examples — there are lots of possible adjustments that might need to be made. If you're struggling and don't know what adjustments need to be made, ask your accountability crew.

The idea is to use your weekly review to see what adjustments need to be made, and set your intentions for the coming week with those adjustments in mind. Then see how it goes in your next weekly review, and continue to adjust if needed.

With these kinds of adjustments, you'll get better and better at the training, and it will become tailored for your life. And it will shift as your life shifts, as you change, as the meaningful work you do changes.

Chapter 14: Falling in Love with the Moment

You are sitting on the earth and you realize that this earth deserves you and you deserve this earth. You are there—fully, personally, genuinely.

~CHÖGYAM TRUNGPA

There was a weekend in 2017 when I was participating in a workshop on intimacy, and a group of men and I had to do a pretty tough physical exercise that made me want to absolutely shut down. We had to raise both arms in the air over our heads, each of us staring deeply into another man's eyes, and keep the arms raised for what seemed like an eternity.

My shoulders and arms started to ache, and I just wanted to quit. The man in front of me gave me an intense stare full of strength and love, and held me in the pose with his gaze. My mind was complaining, screaming that I should put my arms down, rationalizing that it was OK to stop, that this wasn't worth it, that I couldn't do it. But I stayed in the pose.

At one point, with this incredible music playing and my arms screaming and my mind wanting to habitually shut down … I opened to the moment all around me. I took into my awareness the light in the room, the presence of these men doing a deep and powerful practice, the air and trees and life outside the building we were in.

And I fell in love with the moment.

I fell in love with everything around me, the people, the life, the space, the music, the incredible world … and yes, I even fell in love with my discomfort and my poor mind that only wanted to quit.

This experience taught me that we can always open beyond our self-concern, and we can fall in love with the moment, even when it's full of discomfort and uncertainty.

This is the invitation in this Fearless training. To do the training not just because it's good for you, not just to improve, not because you want to be disciplined … but in order to open beyond self-concern and into the beauty of the everchanging moment.

OPENING BEYOND SELF-CONCERN

Most of the time, we are trapped in self-concern. I say this without any judgment — it's just how the human mind works (most of the time). We worry about whether we'll be OK, what others think of us, whether we'll get what we want or be able to avoid what we don't want. We worry about whether things are secure and stable and under our control.

This self-concern is completely natural, but it's not usually very helpful. It traps us into a small world where all we're worried about is ourselves. This training invites us to open to something bigger — something that includes ourselves but also includes a love for others, a desire to serve them, a compassion for their pain. This something bigger might include a world of possibility, of vast openness.

When we get beyond self-concern, the habitual patterns we've been trapped in don't control us as much. We can see that the patterns are just ways to protect that self-concern, but when we become bigger than that, we don't need them anymore. We become absolutely free.

We can open beyond self-concern in any moment. It takes practice, but it's a matter of recognizing when we've closed down in self-concern, and seeing that there is something bigger than that. There is a vast world all around us, full of life and beauty, to be appreciated. There are others who are suffering who could use our compassion.

Opening beyond self-concern can be a physical feeling as well as mental: when you are closed up in self-concern, it can feel like tightness in your torso and head muscles. Opening up beyond that can feel like a relaxing of that tightness, while your awareness broadens to something much more open. Try it now — open your awareness to the wider world around you while relaxing the muscles of your head and torso.

Again, this takes practice. When we open beyond self-concern, we become free. We become our aspirational selves.

FALLING IN LOVE WITH THE MOMENT

Often we reject parts of our experience as "unpleasant," "uncomfortable" or "bad" in some way. We don't want those parts, only the parts we like. We don't want the parts of ourselves we don't like either, just the good parts, please.

What if we accepted all of it? Just relaxed our tight aversion, and accepted it. We don't have to like everything, just accept it. This is a wholesale inclusion of everything, everyone, every part of ourselves. Just relaxing into open and radical acceptance.

The shift this causes is that we no longer have to run from fears, struggles, resistance, uncertainty, discomfort. We no longer have to get control of everything and hope things will change for the better. Things don't have to change — they're just fine, as insecure and uncertain as they might be. We relax into it all, so that we are free from needing to run, avoid, ignore, control.

There is a possibility of getting close to everything, becoming intimate with the moment, and not only accepting what is there but fully appreciating it all for the beauty it has, warts and all.

The invitation is to fully appreciate every single thing about this moment, to witness each moment in its glorious grandeur. To open to this appreciation, as if we were just awakening to a brilliant sunrise.

There is even the possibility of falling in love with the moment. Falling in love doesn't mean that there is nothing we fear, nothing we feel aversion towards. It means that we become intimate with those things we fear and feel aversion about, and feel warmth, love, tenderness toward them. We don't need them to change, because the beauty of this moment includes the sunlight and wind and vibrant life but also includes the fears, struggles, resistance, uncertainty, discomfort. And we wouldn't have it any other way.

Chapter 15: Relaxing into the Openness

One must be deeply aware of the impermanence of the world.

~DOGEN

For the first few years that I started to explore Zen practice, I felt like I didn't quite get it. Sure, sitting in meditation was nice, and helped me develop awareness, but I didn't really understand the teachings on non-duality, impermanence, interdependence, emptiness. The ideas all seemed fine, but I didn't get them on a bodily, experiential level. They didn't shift my reality.

Then a series of things shook me up and I started experiencing a lot more openness. I can't pinpoint it on one particular event — family members were going through serious health challenges, my business was going through changes, we moved homes, a bunch of things happened at once. But they shook up my sense of solidness about the world.

This was unsettling and brought up anxiety in me. The world seemed so ethereal, dreamlike, fluid, unanchored. It was changing constantly, like a never-solid shifting ground under your feet. This troubled me, until I let myself relax into it.

And all of a sudden, the openness of the world felt like freedom.

I started accepting the groundlessness of my life, not as something to fret about or get control over, but as beautifully open, vast and free. Each moment arising from the previous one, begetting a new fluid moment, never fixed, always open possibility. I'm not fixed either. In fact, I'm just a part of an ocean of life, not separate from it all, which is an incredible connection to everything around me that feels so rich and powerful.

That's not to say that I don't return to my old ways of seeing the world — I do, all the time. But I now know that I can open to groundlessness and impermanence and emptiness in a way that is freeing and beautiful.

In this training, the goal isn't just to get stuff done (that's a nice benefit, though). It's not just to get good at being in uncertainty and discomfort (though that's a big part of it). The invitation is to step into openness and experience it as freedom, love, joy.

THE FUNDAMENTAL GROUNDLESSNESS & OPENNESS OF LIFE

The bad news is you're falling through the air,
nothing to hang on to, no parachute.
The good news is there's no ground.

~CHÖGYAM TRUNGPA

Contemplate Chögyam Trungpa's quote for a moment. Think about that — you're falling through the air, no parachute, nothing solid to grab on to. This would usually be enough to send us into panic.

But there's no ground beneath us to crash into. So we're actually completely safe, just without solid ground under our feet, without solidness to cling to. The sane thing to do, then, is to relax. Accept the groundlessness of the situation. Maybe even enjoy it as a beautiful experience.

That's what our life is. It's groundless — we don't control it, we have no certainty, it's impermanent and completely unpredictable in its everchangingness. But that's good news — with nothing fixed, everything is possibility. With nothing certain, we can play and explore. With no control, we can relax and surrender. With nothing predictable, life is an unfolding delightful surprise. We don't want everything to be fixed, predictable, closed. We can be glad that life is open, and bring an attitude of curiosity, play, exploration and adventure.

Most of us are fixed in our ideas — we argue about how we're right and other people are wrong. When we get into a fight with our partner, we get set in being right and let our pride get in the way of an intimate connection. When we want to get healthy, we falter because we're set in our preferences about what we want to eat and how comfortable we should be. When we set out to do meaningful work, we stumble because of fixed ideas as well: people should judge us as successes, we shouldn't fail, we should remain in safety and comfort, we can't change the way we do things.

What if we let go of the fixed ideas and instead opened to curiosity? It would open us to intimate connection, to vulnerability, to healthy changes, to possibility.

Most of us are fixed in our ideas of ourselves. We believe we're separate from everyone else. We believe we're flawed and inadequate. We are fixated on our self-concern.

What if we let go of fixed ideas of ourselves, and opened to the idea that there is no separate self, that we are interdependent with everything else and everyone else around us, co-creating each other, co-arising? You are changed as you read this, because of something I wrote, and I'm changed because you read it. We have co-created each other in this moment, and are not independent of each other. This is happening in everything around us — the trees are "breathing" our carbon dioxide and emitting oxygen for us to breathe, they produce food for us to eat as we produce waste for them to grow, the people around us influence us in countless ways as we influence them, we could not exist without everything around us. We are co-created and co-creating. There is a tremendous dynamic fluidity about this that is never fixed and always open.

You don't have to accept all of that to feel openness in this moment. You can just relax into the fluidity of the groundlessness of it all.

Practice this, and see what might happen if you relax into the vast open possibility of groundlessness.

> *You are consciousness incarnated in the human body, but not limited by it. Consciousness is the clear space of knowing, as vast as the open sky. Rest in consciousness, in loving awareness. Let vastness be your home.*
>
> ~JACK KORNFIELD

Chapter 16: Increasing the Intensity

> *When we find ourselves in a situation in which our buttons are being pushed, we can choose to repress or act out, or we can choose to practice. If we can start to do the exchange, breathing in with the intention of keeping our hearts open to the embarrassment or fear or anger that we feel, then to our surprise we find that we are also open to what the other person is feeling. Open heart is open heart.*

~CHÖGYAM TRUNGPA

Once you've practiced with this method for a bit, you'll start to get the hang of it. You'll get more comfortable with the basic Fearless practice, and start to open to your meaningful work. This is wonderful, but there's always a way to deepen.

To deepen and grow, we find our edge and practice there.

For some people, the edge of their practice is just meditating. It brings up all kinds of discomfort, and they might not be able to do it for a couple minutes without feeling anxious or antsy or unhappy. So they should just practice there, at their edge: meditate for a minute or two, and get used to that.

After awhile, they can practice for a minute or two and it's no problem. Their edge might be 5-10 minutes of meditating. So they practice there until that becomes comfortable. Their edge moves to 15-20 minutes. And so on.

For many of us, our edge is practicing with meaningful work. It can bring up discomfort and anxiety and all of our old patterns. That's the edge we start in with this training — I assume you've meditated a bit and have moved your edge beyond meditating for a couple of minutes.

You train there for awhile, with your edge at doing any kind of meaningful work, and get comfortable there with practice. What's next?

There are ways to find and practice with your edge beyond that. I call them "advanced practices" because they're designed to step up the intensity to increase your stress quickly and get you to your edge so you can practice there.

KEY INSTRUCTIONS (DON'T SKIP)

A few important instructions for advanced practices:

1. These shouldn't be practiced until you've gotten comfortable with the basic Fearless practice and your meaningful work.
2. Start in small doses. Just like meditating for just a couple minutes at first, you don't need to run a marathon when you start. You might only be able to do 10 seconds — that's your edge. That's enough to start.
3. You can increase or decrease intensity as needed to find the right edge for you. You know that the

intensity is too high if you get completely overwhelmed and shut down. You know it's too low if you don't feel any uncertainty, stress, fear, or urge to exit.
4. Be especially sure to practice with gentleness, friendliness, and the fearlessness of being open to what arises. If you haven't cultivated these qualities in your training yet, don't do these practices.

Don't skip these key instructions. They are not optional.

THE ADVANCED PRACTICES

These are not the only possibilities for advanced practices — basically, anything that increases intensity should get you to (or past) your edge. But these are some good examples of what you might try:

- **Do your meaningful work with others**. Start building a collaboration, a partnership, a team. Moving from solo work to leadership is a new level for many people, scarier, more challenging on a number of fronts. If you're just starting in this area, move in small steps rather than immediately leading a huge organization.
- **Do your meaningful work in public**. This book is an example — I'm writing it in public, on a public Google Doc where other people can watch and comment. Writing in public can take a writer to their edge. You can do the same thing for playing music, drawing, coding, teaching, singing, editing videos (via

livestreaming), brainstorming ideas, and many other types of meaningful work.
- **Step up your game, play a bigger game**. Many of us stay in a smaller arena than we're capable of, because it feels safer. That's OK at first, but after you've trained in that arena, your new edge might be in playing a bigger game. This has been true for me in many ways, but I'm stepping out of it and into a bigger mission, a bigger team, a bigger leadership role. How can you challenge yourself to play a bigger game?
- **Hold the ego eradicator pose**. There's a Kundalini yoga pose called Ego Eradicator that is usually paired with "breath of fire" breathing (watch the video) … this is what I was doing when I fell in love with the moment in the story I shared at the beginning of Chapter 14. Hands above your head, holding the pose. I suggest you do this for at least a few minutes, but ideally more than 5 minutes … whatever is required for you to find your edge. The more fit among you can likely do more than 10 minutes — the length you hold the pose is not supposed to be an ego contest, but rather a path to ego eradication. So just hold it until you find your edge … then hold it for a little longer. When you feel stress and discomfort, let yourself open to the uncertainty of the moment, do the basic Fearless practice with whatever you're feeling, notice the urge to quit, and practice with that. Open up to it, relax into the groundlessness, fall in love with the moment.
- **Practice while taking a cold shower (or in icy water)**. I've played around with this practice in the past, but as I write this, it's one of my current daily

practices. I shower in hot water, but at the end of the shower, I switch between very hot and as cold as the shower will go (not cold enough honestly). The idea is not to build up "toughness" or anything like that, but to induce some intensity to a meditation. So while the cold water is flowing over your skin, you can meditate on the sensation of the cold water on skin, but also on the sensation of your resistance and aversion, and watch your thought patterns arise, perhaps wanting to shut down. You can do the basic Fearless practice as you stand in the cold water, you can give yourself compassion, you can relax into the groundlessness, you can fall in love with the moment. Any kind of practice you can do without cold water, you can do with the intensity of the cold. Btw, if you can find a cold plunge at a spa that goes even colder, or create an ice bath, that would increase the intensity. If you live in a place with icy water (a lake, river or pond) … you can practice in this, but only if it's safe and with someone with you in case you have difficulty.

- **Put yourself in greater chaos**. Our lives always have chaos of some kind or another, but sometimes the chaos can feel especially intense. When these moments arise, you can practice with it as an advanced practice, being fully present with the feelings of chaos, the anxiety and stress of it. Opening to the groundless and relaxing into it. Falling in love with it. If you like, you can actually put yourself into greater chaos (if you're not blessed with intense chaos in your life at the moment) — find a busy place like a high-traffic sidewalk, and do work there. Or someplace where you'll be interrupted a lot, or with lots of noise. You can cram your schedule packed with too much to do, and try doing your training in the middle of the pressure to get it all done. The possibilities of putting yourself in chaos are endless. Can you be present with the chaos and open to the groundlessness?

- **Practice in relationship**. Most of the time, we do this training alone, and that can be challenging enough. But practicing in a close relationship adds new levels of complexity to the practice. The trick is to stay open to stress that might arise in your relationship, and when you notice it arising, use it as an opportunity to practice. Be fully with the feelings that arise in you, notice your urge to go to your habitual patterns. Notice how those habitual patterns feel right, feel solid, like they're the right thing to do. Can you stay in the discomfort and uncertainty without running to the patterns? Can you remain in the groundless with curiosity and an open heart, even for a little longer? This practice can transform a relationship if you train wholeheartedly.

- **Find what you've been resisting, and open to it**. Take some time to contemplate what you've been resisting, in any area of your life. Some examples in my life: staying up to date with Slack and other messages, meditating twice a day every single day, logging everything I eat. There's usually some rationalizations for what you're resisting, but not really a good rational reason. So commit to doing one of the things you're resisting, for a week or two, and practice with the resistance and aversion that come up. As you keep your eyes open for what you're resisting, you'll notice more and more of them. The opportunities are everywhere!

- **Face your biggest fears**. Similar to looking for what you've been resisting ... but moving closer to the things that have always induced the greatest fear in you. Things you've known for years, which will always make you say, "Hell no!" What would make the list of your top 3-5 fears? Can you turn towards them, one at a time? Start with the smallest version of the fear — if you're afraid of heights, you just need to get a little higher than you're comfortable with, and practice there with the basic Fearless practice. This is your edge. Then keep moving to greater intensity, always finding your edge. If you are afraid of spiders, can you start by being in the same room as the spider? Then a little closer, a little closer, always finding your edge, until you're right next to the spider. Then touching it (of course, always practice with non-poisonous spiders!). Find your edge, move towards it, practice there.
- **Practice refraining**. This is a similar practice to practicing with what you've been resisting or with your greatest fears ... but the practice is to refrain from what you crave. For example, sweets or checking social media. Set a challenge for yourself to refrain from this craving for a certain amount of time, and then practice with the cravings that come up. Nothing too extreme, just find your edge and practice. The basic practice of refraining is actually practicing with the urge to run to your habitual pattern, which is what we've been practicing in our main training method. When you have the urge to go to your old pattern,

refrain, and just stay present with the urge, the sensations of it. With the uncertainty, being with it. Opening to the groundlessness as you refrain.

Again, we're not limited to these specific practices. The idea is to introduce intensity, chaos and stress so that we can find our edge and practice there, learning to stay open in moments of stress.

> *Meditation is not a matter of trying to achieve ecstasy, spiritual bliss or tranquility, nor is it attempting to be a better person. It is simply the creation of a space in which we are able to expose and undo our neurotic games, our self-deceptions, our hidden fears and hopes.*
>
> ~CHÖGYAM TRUNGPA

Chapter 17: Finding Joy & Gratitude

*Your task is not to seek for love,
but merely to seek and find all the barriers
within yourself that you have built against it.*

~RUMI

When I first started training in uncertainty, I did not enjoy the experience. I found it interesting, but I really didn't want to do it very much, because my old habit was to get away from the certainty and to shut down or try to avoid or control the uncertainty.

But there was a moment I had one day when I was practicing with the uncertainty and suddenly felt grateful that I had the uncertainty. It seemed to me to be a wonderful sign that I was doing something right, that I was doing something meaningful. It became clear to me that I couldn't do anything meaningful at all with this feeling of uncertainty — and that if I didn't feel the uncertainty, it meant I was playing things safe, not really getting out of my comfort zone, not serving people out of love.

And so this practice of feeling the sensations of uncertainty become a clear sign that I was journeying into unknown territory, out of love for those I cared about. I was very grateful for the sensations of groundlessness.

This led me to the idea that I could even be joyful in the middle of the uncertainty, it didn't have to be torture. It didn't have to be burden.

This was a revolutionary idea for me, that this difficult practice of being with my uncertainty could be filled with gratitude and joy!

I began to explore this in a much more open way, and I discovered:

- The more open I was to the feelings of groundlessness, the more I was open to gratitude and joy. Curiosity and welcoming were some of the surest ways for me to open to the groundlessness.
- Whenever I closed out of self-concern (which is natural), I could always find a path to openness if I relaxed and tried to be curious and gentle and friendly.
- The more I brought play into it, the more joyful it became.
- I learned to sense the openness of the situation, an openness that made the situation seem groundless and uncertain. This openness no longer had to be a bad thing — I could see it just as openness, which could feel like freedom, freshness, possibility.
- This idea of possibility become something I played with, and it's pretty transformative — if each moment is not fixed but open then the moment is pure emerging possibility. I can see that openness as endless

> possibility, open to what I'd like to create. I get to
> play, create, transform!

There's no instruction manual for creating joy and gratitude in the middle of your discomfort and uncertainty — it's more of an invitation to explore and play, and see what you can discover.

When you're practicing, instead of seeing it as burden, look for possibility.

Instead of closing in the middle of stress, see if you can remain open, and open your heart. Appreciate the openness of the moment, and find gratitude.

Bring play into the practice, and see if there can be joy at being in this moment of breathtaking beauty and openness.

Chapter 18: Deepening Integrity

Impeccability of the word can lead you to personal freedom, to huge success and abundance; it can take away all fear and transform it into joy and love.

~DON MIGUEL RUIZ

I have a friend who feels his life is a mess — he's behind on all his finances, can't seem to get organized or on top of work, can't find the discipline to meditate or get to the gym, his house is a huge mess, and he feels terrible about himself. In fact, all of this makes him hate himself.

I relate to all of this in so many ways. I struggled for many years just to stick to anything, and for so long my life felt like a complete crapshow. I always felt bad about myself and never felt that I could trust myself to do anything for very long. That changed starting in 2005, when I started to learn to stick to new habits. But even in recent years, there have been things I've had a hard time sticking with.

That changed when I decided to work on deepening my integrity.

The work to deepen my integrity started with honesty: a clear-eyed honesty about whether I was really keeping agreements I made with myself, or my commitments to others. Taking full responsibility for how I was doing with those agreements, without beating myself up.

I did a full assessment: looked at the areas in my life where I wasn't in integrity. I wasn't meditating as consistently as I wanted to. I wasn't staying on top of messages in the communities for my programs. I wasn't as focused on my mission each day as I'd like. I wasn't calling my mom and grandmother (I'm still working on this one). I wasn't taking care of a few things around the house that needed my attention. I wasn't walking every afternoon or as consistent with my exercises as I'd like.

The assessment helped me to get clear on where I was falling short, without any judgment about whether this made me a bad person or not. My self-worth is not based on how I'm doing — I have a basic goodness that I believe in no matter what I do.

So it starts with clarity and honesty, and responsibility without judgment.

BE IMPECCABLE WITH YOUR WORD

In his powerful book, the *Four Agreements*, Toltec shaman Don Miguel Ruiz said that the first and most important of the Four Agreements is to "Be impeccable with your word." He speaks beautifully about the power of the word.

"When you are impeccable, you take responsibility for your actions, but you do not judge or blame yourself," Ruiz writes.

So he says to make an agreement with yourself to *be impeccable with your word.*

This isn't easy, he says: "We have learned to lie as a habit of our communication with others and more importantly with ourselves. We are not impeccable with the word."

But while it isn't easy, he said we can nurture this as a seed of love: "It is up to you to make this agreement with yourself: I am impeccable with my word. Nurture this seed, and as it grows in your mind, it will generate more seeds of love to replace the seeds of fear."

The results are nothing less than magical: "Just this one agreement can change your whole life. Impeccability of the word can lead you to personal freedom, to huge success and abundance; it can take away all fear and transform it into joy and love."

I believe absolutely in this agreement.

HOW TO DEEPEN INTEGRITY

What we learn as we dive deeper into integrity work in our lives is that it is Fearless practice. As we look at where we're not in integrity, we look at why. And the answer is fear, old patterns, rationalizations, resistance. All of our old friends!

We can work with what comes up, as we start to get into integrity, in the same way we've been training. As I try to meditate more consistently, I can see that I feel resistance and that I'm rationalizing, and so I can do the basic Fearless practice around these patterns.

The key is to **take full responsibility**. We have to stop believing our rationalizations, stop blaming everything else, and take 100% responsibility for our lives.

Full responsibility means:

- Being clear and honest about where we're falling short
- Admit when we're wrong
- Noticing what effects being out of integrity has on us and the people around us
- Figuring out what it takes to get into integrity
- Do the basic Fearless practice with whatever fears and resistance and rationalizations are getting in the way
- Noticing what effects being back in integrity has on us and the people around us

So we're not beating ourselves up because it's OK that we failed, it's OK to be wrong. **These failures actually help us build integrity**, because if we were always right and everything were always good and easy, integrity would be easy. Failing helps us to strengthen and deepen our integrity.

Integrity means that we accept and love all of ourselves, not just the "good" parts. We become intimate with the parts we've seen as ugly for so long, and start to befriend them. This is the only way to move into complete integrity, out of love for ourselves, not hiding from the parts we don't want to see.

Integrity, then, means **being willing to be vulnerable**. If we are always protecting ourselves with defenses, we can never admit when we're wrong, admit when we've failed, admit that we're ashamed. If we can't admit these things, we can't really be fully honest — which means we're not in integrity. We have to be willing to be vulnerable to be authentic, to be honest, to be living in integrity.

There's no one path to integrity, but I believe that as we deepen our integrity, we must bring honesty, vulnerability, responsibility, love for ourselves, and the willingness to get close to all parts of ourselves, even the ones that are scared and that fail.

BE WILLING TO WALK THROUGH WALLS

If we are to deepen our purpose, we need to deepen our intention and deepen our integrity, our willingness to be impeccable with our word.

We can't say that we have a purpose in this world, to serve others with our deepest love, and then neglect to uphold that intention. **Purpose and integrity must be married**.

To paraphrase one of my teachers, we need to **become a person who would walk through walls to achieve their mission**. Think about this image: there is nothing that would stop you, because of how committed you are to your purpose.

How do we deepen our commitment so that we would walk through walls?

We resolve that there is nothing more important than this one purpose, and that we will give our entire selves to this. We contemplate the hearts that we are serving through this mission, and decide that they are more important than our discomfort, than our rationalizations, than our old stories and habits. We become absolutely clear that we will be impeccable with our word, including our word to ourselves that we will achieve this mission.

We become single-minded in focus. This is the one thing that we will focus on in the next few years, the one goal that we have for this year, the one thing that we are trying to accomplish this month, the single most important thing I'm going to accomplish today.

And we fail at all of that. **Failure will help us deepen into commitment and integrity**, because we are not going to turn away when we fail, but instead get closer to the failure, be with it, practice fearlessly with it, become intimate with the failure, and use it to grow.

This is how we become the person who would walk through walls for our mission, and the person who is committed to being impeccable with their word.

Chapter 19: Deepening Focus

*Concentrate all your thoughts upon the work at hand.
The sun's rays do not burn until brought to a focus.*

~ALEXANDER GRAHAM BELL

My oldest son told me the other day that he noticed that all of the successful people he has admired seem to have one thing in common: they pour everything they have into a single focus until it's achieved. They might have multiple passions and goals over a number of years, but it always seems to be one at a time.

There are exceptions to this, of course, but it feels like a powerful truth to me. Focus on one thing at a time, pour your entire being into it, and the results will be much more powerful.

If we are to deepen our pursuit of purpose, this kind of incredible focus should be cultivated.

Unfortunately, our world is set up for anything but focus. Technology is a wonderful and magical thing, but tech companies are motivated to get and keep your attention as much as they can. And they are very good at it. They've learned how to get you coming back, how to tap into the human psyche like no one has before. Television, which was seen as an evil technology for decades by some people, seems like an amateur in comparison now.

So we're surrounded by an environment of technology that is designed to grab our attention. Our focus is fragmented and we are finding it increasingly difficult to find the focus to read longer writing or do tasks that require focus. We are training our minds in distraction and procrastination.

And yet, to do our meaningful work, we need to find focus. Anything meaningful will require a greater amount of focus in a single session, and grater single-minded focus over time.

How can we deepen our focus so that we are creating the world we'd like?

We can cultivate a deeper focus, but it must start with a recognition that our time is precious and limited.

RESOLVE TO MAKE THE MOST OF TIME

> *Students today should begrudge every moment of time. This dewlike life fades away; time speeds swiftly. In this short life of ours, avoid involvement in superfluous things and just study the Way.*
>
> ~DOGEN

I remember when I was in my 20s, and time always felt like a (basically) unlimited resource. Intellectually, I knew that I would die someday and that my years were limited, but it felt so far away that I didn't need to worry about it.

I've come to realize that this is one of the fundamental mistakes most of us make. Every day. We waste our days in distraction because it doesn't really feel like it matters. But ask my dad if it matters — he died unexpectedly 4 years ago, and while he was an extraordinarily talented artist, he procrastinate a lot, and probably only painted a fraction of the great art he could have created.

Our days matter. It helps to start at the end, as Stephen Covey suggested in his seminal book, *The 7 Habits of Highly Effective People*. He invited us to visualize our own funeral — to think about what we'd like said about us at the end. How do we want to have lived the years of our lives? It's also helpful to think about how limited those years will have been — we don't know how many it will be, but we know they're limited.

We could die tomorrow, next year, a decade from now, or a few decades. It's unknown, but limited. This is nothing to despair about, but just to remind ourselves that our days are precious and limited, and worth making the most of.

The Stoic philosopher Seneca said, ""It's not at all that we have too short a time to live, but that we squander a great deal of it."

We have enough days. We just need to make them count.

FOCUS ON A SINGLE GOAL

In the book *The One Thing*, author Gary Keller drives home the idea that if we put all of our focus into one thing that truly matters, we will create much more incredible results.

This idea of narrowing down to one single goal doesn't come naturally to me. I am a man of many ambitions, and I'm notoriously optimistic about how much I can get done. I think I can do more than one goal well, by splitting up my day or week, and I think I can maintain focus on many things. But it's very rarely true — I've very often taken on too much, resulting in not being able to meet deadlines, not delivering as I say I will, not doing very well on my goals. And on multiple occasions, it's resulting in me having to kill projects, hurting those who were counting on me.

This is painful. To let people down, to hurt them if I have to fire them, to achieve mediocre results … these are painful results from a habit of trying to do too much. Last year, this all became very clear to me — I got clear that I was hurting myself and others by taking on way too much. My optimism and habit to grab every project and goal in sight was not sustainable.

Keller's book *The One Thing* really resonates with this clear insight. He talks about Extreme Pareto Principle — if the Pareto Principle is that 20% of actions get 80% of our results, then we can take it further by looking at the most important 20% of the 20%, and then find the most important 20% of that 20% … until we figure out **the one action or one goal that matters most**, that will make the biggest impact.

Keller's One Thing goal setting system is deceptively simple and powerful. You start with your one most important long-term goal, and work down to the one task you should be working on right now:

- **Someday Goal**: What's the One Thing I want to do someday? (or your biggest long-term goal)
- **Five-Year Goal**: Based on my Someday Goal, what's the One Thing I can do in the next five years?
- **One-Year Goal**: Based on my Five-Year Goal, what's the One Thing I can do this year?
- **Monthly Goal**: Based on my One-Year Goal, what's the One Thing I can do this month?
- **Weekly Goal**: Based on my Monthly Goal, what's the One Thing I can do this week?
- **Daily Goal**: Based on my Weekly Goal, what's the One Thing I can do today?
- **Right Now Goal**: Based on my Daily Goal, what's the One Thing I can do right now?

Using this simple system, you can figure out the single most important thing you should be doing right now to accomplish your mission in life. I invite you to work through these questions and write down your one goal for each level.

And then block off your time each day to get your One Thing done, and to become singularly focused.

CULTIVATING FOCUS ON A SINGLE TASK

*When you do something,
you should burn yourself up completely,
like a good bonfire, leaving no trace of yourself.*

~SHUNRYU SUZUKI

What we put in front of us to give our attention to, to give our life energy to, is a sacred choice.

If you choose to read an article or browse through social media or reply to messages, you are deciding to use some of your precious, limited time alive on that task. That is a gift you are giving, a chunk of your life. Your attention and effort has power, and can change the world.

Most of us choose to spend this power very casually, randomly choosing tasks and things to look at online. But what would it be like to be deliberate about what we put in front of ourselves? What would it be like to treat the task in front of us as sacred, worthy of our full attention and love?

If we are to push deeply into purpose, it would be helpful to cultivate a deeper focus on the task before us. This increases our power to accomplish our meaningful work, and the mission we have set before us in the world.

To be willing to walk through walls means we must cultivate a sacred focus.

This comes with practice. **We can bring attention to how we're spending our attention** — are we jumping around, switching between tabs, popping in and out of various messaging apps? Or are we staying with the important task in front of us? Pay attention to this throughout the day, and start to cultivate the commitment to stay.

We can treat the singularly important task in front of us as a sacred activity. If I'm going to sit down to write, for example, am I just casually starting the writing or do I bring a sense of devotion to the writing task? That means elevating it to something worthy of devotion, worthy of our full love and full presence. What would it be like to treat each important task as an act of devotion?

We can treat each sacred task as a meditation. In sitting meditation, we cultivate the ability to stay, treating this moment as worthy of our complete attention. We might get pulled away by thoughts, get hooked by a particularly powerful storyline, but we practice noticing that and then coming back. We can do the same kind of practice with the sacred task in front of us — practice opening up in full presence to the task, and then practice noticing when our attention is pulled away and then coming back. Every sacred task becomes an opportunity to practice, with devotion.

We can treat every sacred task as an act of love. If our meaningful work is a way to serve people we care deeply about, then each meaningful task is an act of love for those people. We can start the sacred task by setting an intention to serve them, keeping their hearts in our heart. And then let the love pour out of us as we work with devotion and focus.

What would it be like to cultivate this way of being with our sacred tasks?

> *One reason so few of us achieve what we truly want is that we never direct our focus; we never concentrate our power. Most people dabble their way through life, never deciding to master anything in particular.*
>
> ~TONY ROBBINS

Chapter 20: Deepening into Emptiness

*Spiritual awakening is exactly dropping
the sense of one's narrow separateness.*

~NORMAN FISCHER

One of the deepest teachings of Zen and Tibetan Buddhism (among others) is the idea of interdependence and impermanence. It is often called "emptiness," but this is a difficult-to-understand word in English.

It is at heart a very simple concept that is best experienced rather than explained … but let's try to summarize it simply:

- Things exist, but they don't exist as independent selves — they are said to be "empty" of independent existence, which is what "emptiness" refers to (not non-existence, but non-separate-existence).
- Rather than independent, everything is interdependent — we are all existing because of everything around us. Buddhist author Thich Nhat Hanh calls this "interbeing," because we exist interdependently with everything else.

- He describes a cloud existing in a piece of paper — because a cloud produced the rain that watered the tree that was turned into the paper. The paper also has the logger that cut down the tree, the soil and other beings that went into the tree's growth, the sun that gave the tree (and everything else) energy, the wheat that went into the bread that the logger ate for food, the logger's mother and teacher and so on and so on.
- In the same way, in my existence is everything else that caused me to be in existence, and everything that caused those things to be in existence, and so on.
- This creates a web of interconnections, but it also means that we are all co-creating everything and are co-created by everything. We co-arise along with everything else.
- All of our ideas about this thing being a "tree" and that being a "person" and so on are just ideas, empty of true existence, because the tree isn't just a tree, it is everything that helped it to come into existence. In each moment, a new version of us arises only because everything else made it possible. So our ideas about everything are not solid, just conceptions without real nature.
- If this is true, then we can let go of those ideas and just take in the very fluid and unfixed nature of everything in this moment. Things are not so solid, but rather open and dynamic in nature.

That is a long way of saying that the nature of reality is open, vast, unfixed, fluid, impermanent and constantly changing, groundless, fresh, ungraspable.

And far from emptiness feeling sad, lifeless, or meaningless … this way of seeing the "the true nature of things and events" (as the Dalai Lama put it) is rich, dynamic, connected and beautiful.

We resist uncertainty and groundlessness because we want stability, but if we dive into this experience of emptiness and interconnected openness, we can see groundlessness as good news.

It's good news because if we can open to the flux and fluidity of the world, we don't have to grasp, don't have to push things away, and don't have to suffer as much — we can relax into the openness. We can rest in the interconnectedness, which can feel like home, like love. As Suzuki Roshi said, "Emptiness is like being at your mother's bosom and she will take care of you."

It is liberating in its vast openness, fresh in its never-fixed moment-to-moment emerging.

WAKING UP TO OUR TRUE NATURE

Enlightenment for a wave in the ocean is the moment the wave realises that it is water.

~THICH NHAT HANH

Imagine that you are a wave in the ocean. You rise up above the rest of the water, look around at all the water and the rest of the waves around you … and you think, "Wow, what a huge ocean, but I feel so alone, and also I wonder what the other waves think of me, and also I hope I can become the biggest and best wave!"

This is how we are as human beings, looking around at everyone and everything else, thinking we are separate. Feeling lonely and inadequate. Worrying about what people will think of us. Hoping we achieve some kind of recognition or greatness. Looking out for our self-concern.

But we are water in a vast ocean! We just need to wake up to that reality. When we do, we can see that in fact, we are connected to everything, and this is a return to the wholeness that we long for. We cannot be inadequate because we are always whole. We cannot be lonely, we are together with everything else. We don't have to grasp, because there's nothing to grasp onto. We don't have to worry about our self-concern, because it's not a real thing.

We become whole, interconnected, fluid and open. Or rather, we wake up to this fact, because it's already true, even if we don't realize it.

How do we wake up to this reality? We drop our ideas. Every conception we have of others, of ourselves, of what others think of us or have done to us, of what we want or don't like … we drop these ideas. Instead, we learn to feel pure experience. Pure experience has no boundaries or form, it's just experience. We drop conceptions and just experience, moment to moment.

This is open, free, everchanging. It's groundlessness, openness, uncertain and unconstricted.

We can open to this reality in meditation, or in any moment, when we just drop into pure experience. Our ideas, thoughts and conceptions will assert themselves (as old habits tend to do), and we can just see them as arising phenomena, empty of any kind of true nature, just dreams. Then drop back into pure experience, which is fluid and unconstrained.

We can rest in this vast openness, this groundlessness, and learn to love it. It is a return to wholeness, our basic goodness.

This goes beyond our desire to accomplish our goals, which many of you might have had in mind when you started this book. It's a deeper way of practicing with groundlessness, but as you practice it, you start to awaken to the incredible nature of reality, in small glimpses but then more and more as you continue to practice. You fall in love with the heartbreaking beauty of the moment, as ungraspable and uncontainable as it is.

> *A wave on the ocean has a beginning and an end, a birth and a death. But Avalokiteshvara tells us that the wave is empty. The wave is full of water, but it is empty of a separate self. A wave is a form that has been made possible, thanks to the existence of wind and water. If a wave only sees its form, with its beginning and end, it will be afraid of birth and death. But if the wave sees that it is water and identifies itself with the water, then it will be emancipated from birth and death. Each wave is born and is going to die, but the water is free from birth and death.*
>
> ~THICH NHAT HANH

Chapter 21: Cultivating Mastery of Purpose

> *Do not think that what is hard for you to master is humanly impossible; and if it is humanly possible, consider it to be within your reach.*
>
> ~MARCUS AURELIUS

This book is just the start of the training in groundlessness, openness, and deep purpose. This is a neverending journey, with constant deepening, growth, learning.

My friend (and former coach) Toku McCree describes mastery as a mountain with no peak — you keep climbing it without ever reaching the destination. And yet, the attitude is just to keep going, without despairing, do the training for the sake of the training itself. It's not a means to an end, but an opening to the profoundness of the moment.

What we are learning here is how to transform our relationship with the world. We struggle with habitual patterns because our relationship in the past has been fraught with not wanting, with grasping, with seeking of comfort and hiding from fear. I say this without judgment but love, because we have only wanted to protect our tender hearts and find happiness. But we've learned that this way of being in the world only gets us so far — our intelligence and good intentions and competency can overcome mountains, but at some point they stop being enough to overcome the inner mountains we're facing.

So we move into this training, trying to find a way to move these inner mountains. We dive into the training, maybe with some trepidation at going into the deep end, not sure if we're up to the task. We begin to learn about ourselves in the process, and we start to shift how we relate to our fears, our feelings, our experience in the moment. This opens up a powerful transformation.

But this isn't the end — in this transformation, we start to get glimpses of openness that feel like freedom and joy. This might not be something we can do all the time, but the glimpses open us up. We begin practicing with that and find even more powerful transformation, the more we practice.

That's not the end either — we can always go deeper. We begin to find clarity, to understand how this all works, and find fluency. With more practice and exploration, there are greater and greater degrees of mastery. We launch into the path of the Bodhisattva, which is to transform ourselves so that we can transform others, to devote ourselves to a loving path of helping all beings. This requires even deeper practice, and we discover new levels of mastery. Even then, there's no end to the path.

We find that we can use anything to transform us. We move closer to pain, to death, to addiction, to despair and depression, to hatred and violence, and discover that intimacy with any of these can be a powerful path of transformation as well. There's no end to the deepening.

We let our tender hearts be open to the world, let our hearts be broken by the sadness, pain and beauty of the world, let ourselves be vulnerable and intimate with others, with ourselves, with the world. There is no end to this path of mastery.

> *To be a spiritual warrior, one must have a broken heart; without a broken heart and the sense of tenderness and vulnerability, your warriorship is untrustworthy.*
>
> ~CHÖGYAM TRUNGPA

HOW TO CULTIVATE CONTINUED MASTERY

> *When we train our mind to embrace what's hard instead of trying to get rid of it, we have begun to walk a path of growth, happiness, and true resilience.*
>
> ~NORMAN FISCHER

The key idea to keep in mind is that there is nothing that can knock us off the path. Every single obstacle, every single failure, every single discouragement and quitting and closing and heartbreak … is exactly the path we need to be on. It's exactly what we need to practice on. It's exactly what we need to get closer to.

So mastery starts with simply opening ourselves to whatever we encounter on the path. If you are confused and don't think you're getting it, that's perfect — you can open your heart and move closer to your confusion and lack of clarity, to your fear and resistance. If you fail to practice and feel guilty about it, feel inadequate, that's also perfect — you can let your heart be opened by the pain of failing and pain of inadequacy, let yourself feel these struggles and let yourself feel connected to every other person who struggles with these as well.

We can let ourselves open to any pain, any struggle, any failure, any fear. We can tell ourselves that this is too hard, and then open up and embrace that. Each time we do, we are training ourselves to embrace the struggle, the difficulty, the discomfort, the fear the pain. This is how we start to cultivate resilience into our path of mastery.

We have to let go of the idea that this learning process resembles anything close to a linear process. It's much messier, much richer. You start out not knowing what you're doing, but you stumble around confusedly. Then you try again, and again, until you start to get a feel for it. You keep practicing, with this newfound sense of feel, and get better and better each time you come back. You get set back, and then come back, and this time it's a different experience because of the setback. Each setback changes you, each return changes you. Every time you come back to the practice, you are a different person, and you learn something new because you've changed, like viewing the same painting in a museum many times over a lifetime. You come closer and closer to mastery, because you are constantly deepening your learning, changed by the constant coming back. It's not linear but messy, because that's how learning and growth work.

Notice when you are seeking a sense of solidity to your mastery. Lots of times, when we're learning something, we want to master it so that we don't feel like a novice anymore. It's shaky to feel like a novice, not knowing what you're doing. We want the solid ground of feeling like we know what we're doing. That's not what mastery is about — it's about continually putting yourself in the place of shakiness, of the beginner's mind of seeing things afresh, not knowing exactly what you're doing or how it works. Even when you start to feel like you know what you're doing, you move into shakiness on purpose, pushing your edge, finding new things you don't know. Admitting you don't know exactly how something works is where new learning begins, even after years of learning about something. Put yourself in that shaky place of not knowing, whenever you feel like you're trying to put solid ground under your feet.

MOVE TOWARD DIFFICULTY, RESISTANCE, PAIN

The tendency of most people is to move away from things that are difficult or painful. When we practice, this tendency shows itself in staying with the skills we feel comfortable with. When we get decent at a skill, we tend to keep practicing it, and ignore the parts of our training that are hard. We move away from resistance.

But to walk the path of mastery, we have to move toward the resistance, and lean into anything that is painful or difficult. That's the path of fearlessness.

Robert Greene, from his book *Mastery*, says that we should adopt Resistance Practice if we are to attain mastery.

"The principle is simple—you go in the opposite direction of all of your natural tendencies when it comes to practice. First, you resist the temptation to be nice to yourself. You become your own worst critic; you see your work as if through the eyes of others. You recognize your weaknesses, precisely the elements you are not good at. Those are the aspects you give precedence to in your practice. You find a kind of perverse pleasure in moving past the pain this might bring. Second, you resist the lure of easing up on your focus. You train yourself to concentrate in practice with double the intensity, as if it were the real thing times two. In devising your own routines, you become as creative as possible. You invent exercises that work upon your weaknesses. You give yourself arbitrary deadlines to meet certain standards, constantly pushing yourself past perceived limits. In this way you develop your own standards for excellence, generally higher than those of others."

With this kind of Resistance Practice, he says, we can accomplish more in 5 hours of intense practice than most people achieve in 10. More than that, I've found that by practicing with what we resist, we develop the skill of not shying away from the parts that we're afraid of. This is indispensable as we climb the mountain of mastery.

Chapter 22: The Training Program

> *If we're willing to give up hope that insecurity and pain can be eliminated, then we can have the courage to relax with the groundlessness of our situation. This is the first step on the path.*
>
> ~PEMA CHODRON

When you're ready to start training, it's time to set up your structure and create a training program for yourself. If you'd like to go deeper and practice with me and dozens of others, please consider joining my Fearless Training Program. It's the best way to structure this training and get the support to go deeper.

Here's the program I recommend that you set up for yourself:

1. **Deliberate on your deep purpose**. Read Chapter 5 and get clear with your deep purpose (sitting in stillness until you get that clarity). Read Chapter 6 and get clear on who you care deeply about (other than family & friends) — these are the people you are serving with love with your meaningful work.
2. **Set a goal for your meaningful work each month, with a review at the end of the month**. What goal would you like to set for your meaningful work this month? The goal isn't set in stone, but something to

aim for. Have a reminder to do a review for how you did at the end of the month.

3. **Choose something you can do every day, as a practice**. Now convert the monthly goal into a daily activity. Write every day for 30 minutes. Record or edit a video each day. Call 3 potential clients. This activity isn't the training itself, it's the training ground, to see what uncertainty comes up. If the activity doesn't give you uncertainty, you're playing too small a game — be bolder and step up the game.

4. **Have a group of people holding your intention (your accountability crew), and check in with them weekly**. Ask at least several other people to hold you accountable not only to your goal but your training intentions. Ideally, it's other people doing the training — for this, I recommend my Fearless Training Program. The key is to share your intentions with them, let them hold those intentions in their hearts, and then feel solidly committed to them. And check in every week on a certain day (Monday, for example) — report how you did with your intentions, what victories you had, what struggles, what you learned. What pattern is showing up? What have you seen shift? Then share your intentions for the coming week. In this way, you'll learn and be able to adjust your training.

5. **Pick a time and place, and carefully consider your physical environment**. If you are going to write, when and where are you going to write? Where will you be when you call potential clients or record videos? Consider how the physical environment will affect the training — do you want to shut off the

Internet, play music, have tea, clear the space, turn off your phone? Pick a time and try to do the training every day at that time. If something comes up to interfere with doing it at that time, consciously pick another time to do it. But don't give in to your rationalizations.

6. **Do your meaningful work as your training, and practice with the uncertainty that comes up**. At the time and place you set for your training, do the task you set for yourself. If you feel like putting it off, notice what you have an urge to do instead (your pattern). Instead of indulging in the pattern, train with the feeling of uncertainty that comes up. (More on the specifics of this training in the next chapter.) Maybe you are doing it but feel like switching. Notice this, practice with the uncertainty. Maybe you're doing it but not liking it, complaining about it, dreading it. Notice this and practice.

7. **Make note of the habitual patterns that come up, or have others call them out for you**. As you attempt to do your meaningful work in each practice session, you'll start to notice your old patterns arising. That's good news! Now you can get clear on the patterns. If you don't see the patterns, talk to someone else about it, let them ask you questions, and then let them honestly and lovingly call out the patterns.

8. **Shift your pattern by repeatedly staying in the uncertainty instead of running**. As you become clear on your pattern, you'll see it more and more clearly. You'll be aware when you have the urge to indulge in the pattern. Instead, stay in the uncertainty,

stay in the discomfort of not running, and after continued training in this, you will shift the pattern.
10. **Collect & acknowledge your victories**. Each week, note the small and large victories you've had. Celebrate them, and acknowledge your wholehearted efforts. At the end of each month, look back on your weekly check-ins and list your victories for the month. After a few months, list all your victories in one place. These shifts are worth noting.
11. **Continued mastery: constant deepening**. The program above will cause tremendous shifts over the course of 3-6 months, and even more over a year. But this is a lifelong training in mastery. To continue to deepen, every 2-3 months, look at the areas for continued mastery below. See if you can dive into them and explore them more deeply than you have before.

AREAS FOR CONTINUED MASTERY

Some areas to explore on a regular basis, for continued mastery, were suggested in individual chapters:

- **Working with your obstacles**: Find the obstacles that have been getting in the way, and then focus on them as your training ground. If you're resisting something, rationalizing, trying to grasp for control — use that as an area to train with, as you path for growth.
- **Adjusting the training**: This should actually be a regular practice, to look at ways you might need to adjust your training. Each week, and especially each

month, review and see if there are any difficulties that require an adjustment to your method (time, place, how you're practicing, accountability, etc.).
- **Falling in love with the moment, relaxing into openness, finding joy & gratitude**: See the individual chapters on each of these for more. Each of these could be a focus for a month, for how you're training with your meaningful work.
- **Deepening integrity**: How well are you sticking to what you said you're going to do? Do the work around integrity in the chapter on this topic. How willing are you to walk through walls to accomplish your mission? You can revisit your commitment level and deepen it on a regular basis.
- **Deepening focus**: Reflect on how much time you have left in life, and resolve to make the most of it. Review whether you have a single-minded focus on your mission. Practice deepening your focus on a single task.
- **Deepening into emptiness**: After about six month of practice with this program, you might start to explore this deeper topic. It's not always easy to grasp, especially if you haven't been practicing with mindfulness for very long (or even if you have!). But it's an amazing area to explore, as an experiential (not intellectual) practice. I recommend that you keep coming back to this topic, as it will become clearer and clearer over time.

If that seems like a lot of work, don't get overwhelmed. Or rather, practice with your feeling of overwhelm. Focus on one thing at a time, and look at all of these areas as wonderful playgrounds to explore. You have lots of adventures awaiting you.

THE FEARLESS TRAINING PROGRAM

If you'd like to solidify your structure and get the support you need for this kind of training, I highly recommend you join the Fearless Training Program.

Here's what the program provides:

1. **Small teams**: We have small groups of 5-10 people who support each other, do live group calls, check in with each other daily or weekly, help call out each other's patterns.
2. **Monthly focuses**: Each month, we focus on a way to practice. This monthly focus includes videos, articles, homework, and the live call and meditation training mentioned below. Over the months, we explore some amazing practices!
3. **Monthly live training call**: Each month, we do a live call with the whole community (in addition to the small team calls). We do a talk and training on the monthly topic, and then dive into questions or problems you might have.
4. **Meditation trainings**: I record a new meditation training each month, to be listened to and practiced with all month long (and beyond, if you like).
5. **Library of content**: There's a large and growing library of content — training articles and videos, meditation trainings, recordings of the training calls and 1-on-1 coaching calls I've done, and more.

6. **Weekly check-ins**: Each week, we hold each other accountable with a weekly check-in, where you review your past week's wins and struggles and what you've learned, and then set your intentions for the next week. This is to keep you on track and help you adjust your training regularly.
7. **Bonuses**: We include a 100% discount for the Habit Mastery Course, and four bonus ebooks: Essential Zen Habits, The Habit Guide, Ultralight: Zen Habits Guide to Traveling Light, and the Zen Habits Beginner's Guide to Mindfulness.

You can try the program free for a week, then $49/month after that. Check it out here:

fearless.zenhabits.net

INDEBTEDNESS & ACKNOWLEDGEMENTS

This book wasn't written by one person — it was compiled by me, but developed by thousands.

To start with, there's my Zen teacher, Zesho Susan O'Connell. And the lineage of teachers before her, from Tenshin Reb Anderson (who I've learned so much from) to the ancestors and Bodhisattvas that came before him.

I must also acknowledge Pema Chödrön and her teacher Chögyam Trungpa Rinpoche, who both taught me many of the ideas in this training. I've never studied under them, but consider them my teachers nonetheless.

I should acknowledge another of my teachers, John Wineland, for his teachings on purpose and holding the pose that have influenced me greatly. My friend and former coach Toku McCree has been a wonderful influence on me as well.

Coyote Jackson is a member of my team and a big factor in the success of the Fearless Training Program, and a teacher of mine in the art of basic goodness.

I wrote this book with all the members of the Fearless Training Program in my heart, and they have been a huge part in the creation of this training and the development of these practices. They've co-created this with me and Coyote.

Thousands of members of my Sea Change Program and readers of Zen Habits have been a big part of my journey and have influenced me in a countless number of ways. I can't credit them individually but they have shaped me and my mission. They too have been in my heart, along with, as always, my loving family.

> *Be kind to your sleeping heart.*
> *Take it out into the vast fields of light...*
> *And let it breathe.*
>
> ~HAFEZ

Printed in Great Britain
by Amazon